81 QUESTIONS
FOR PARENTS

81 QUESTIONS FOR PARENTS

Helping Your Kids Succeed in School

KRISTEN J. AMUNDSON

ROWMAN & LITTLEFIELD
Lanham • Boulder • New York • London

Published by Rowman & Littlefield
An imprint of The Rowman & Littlefield Publishing Group, Inc.
4501 Forbes Boulevard, Suite 200, Lanham, Maryland 20706
www.rowman.com

6 Tinworth Street, London, SE11 5AL, United Kingdom

British Library Cataloguing in Publication Information Available

Library of Congress Cataloging-in-Publication Data

Names: Amundson, Kristen J., author.
Title: 81 questions for parents : helping your kids succeed in school / Kristen J.
  Amundson.
Other titles: Eighty one questions for parents
Description: Lanham : Rowman & Littlefield, [2021] | Includes bibliographical
  references. | Summary: "This book provides answers to parents everyday
  questions regarding school."—Provided by publisher.
Identifiers: LCCN 2020049969 (print) | LCCN 2020049970 (ebook) | ISBN
  9781475859348 (cloth) | ISBN 9781475859355 (epub)
Subjects: LCSH: Education—Parent participation.
Classification: LCC LB1048.5 .A47 2021 (print) | LCC LB1048.5 (ebook) |
  DDC 372.119/2—dc23
LC record available at https://lccn.loc.gov/2020049969
LC ebook record available at https://lccn.loc.gov/2020049970

To parents everywhere:
your job was hard even before the global pandemic!

CONTENTS

ACKNOWLEDGMENTS

It seems appropriate somehow to talk about a book on parenting by discussing its gestation period, which was long. During the many years that I thought about writing about parents and schools, I was also seeing and living the parent–school relationship from both sides. It took a global pandemic to give me the time and space to sit down and get all those fleeting thoughts and observations on paper.

The late John Wherry, founder of the Parent Institute, started me on the path to writing about parents and schools. His unwavering belief that kids learn best when parents and schools work together has guided my work ever since.

Tom Koerner and everyone at Rowman & Littlefield have been so generous in giving me the opportunity to write about what I have learned over the years. I'm grateful for our partnership.

Thanks to everyone who so shared their time and their insights in interviews. Lindsay Arnold, Lindsay Dworkin, Stacey Finkel, Elena Guarinello, Paige Kowalski, Renee Lang, Lynn Mitchell, Eleanor Saslaw, and Eric and Janet Soller, your experiences will help make the hard work of parenting a little easier.

An earlier version of this book was tentatively titled *How Band Can Get Your Kid Into Harvard* and would have highlighted the Kids of Note program described in Chapter 6. I am so proud of all the students in that program—Jonathan and Genesis Amaya, Oscar Castro-Paz, Astrid Garcia, Camilo Rodriguez, and John Rey and Justin Tangaran. And of course I owe a huge debt of gratitude to Kristi Thomas, whose Teacher of the Year Award was richly deserved and whose dedication to kids seemingly knows no limits.

My sister Sue Ellingsen and my godson Andrew Ellingsen were much more than just expert sources for the book. They were supporters and cheerleaders and providers of great wisdom.

Some portions of this book appeared in my other parenting publications, including *Getting Your Child Ready for Kindergarten* and *Kids Don't Come With Instruction Manuals.*

I am grateful to my daughter Sara, who was basically my living experiment in parenting and has only rarely reminded me of the times I fell short of the mark. Being Sara's mother has been the greatest and most rewarding adventure of my life. (I owe her special thanks for the early edits and occasional reminders that I just had to quit whining and start writing.)

But most of all I want to thank all the parents over the years who trusted me to make policy affecting their children, who read my parenting advice and told me it was helpful, and who showed me in their interactions with their children's schools that we truly can make education better for all kids.

INTRODUCTION

This is not exactly the book I planned to write. For years, I'd thought about writing a book addressed to the desperate parents who were terrified that their high school senior would not get accepted into any college and would end up living in their basement. They started worrying in kindergarten—should they hold their child out for a year? They worried through elementary school—could they ever ask for a specific teacher? They worried in middle school, but of course every parent worries through middle school. And then all that angst and agita just exploded when their child reached high school.

I figured I had a story to tell. I'm a former teacher who spent nearly a decade on the school board of one of the nation's finest public school systems—Fairfax County, Virginia. Even more important than those professional qualifications, I'm the parent of a child who did receive fat envelopes from some of the nation's most selective colleges and universities, including Princeton, from which she graduated. I also helped students from a wide range of backgrounds, including immigrants whose parents never completed middle school, successfully apply to excellent colleges where they received significant financial aid.

Over the years, parents stopped me on the street (or in the grocery store or even—as God is my witness—in the communion line) to ask questions. Did their kid need to take algebra in eighth grade (yes). Was it a problem that they weren't reading at the start of first grade (no). Was it a problem that they still weren't reading in third grade (yes).

But probably the most common question I got over the years was, "What can we do to help our child in this increasingly competitive environment?" I always gave parents the same answer.

Band, I'd tell them. Enroll your child in the band.

Year after year, I shared this advice—and other hard-earned lessons about how to get the very best education for your child in *any* school in the country—with frantic parents. Often, these parents told me, "You really ought to write a book."

Then two things changed the whole shape of what I was writing. First, the Varsity Blues scandal exposed the steps affluent parents were willing to take to get their kids accepted into a selective university. I knew I didn't want to write anything that would fuel even more pressure to adopt that insane (and as it turned out, felonious) behavior. But I knew parents were still struggling to help their high school senior find—and be accepted at—the right college.

And then, of course, there was COVID-19. In the spring of 2020, parents across the United States found themselves quarantined with kids who suddenly had to start going to school online. Parents who were themselves trying to figure out how to log onto a Zoom meeting found themselves also trying to help one child with long division and another with the life cycle of a butterfly. The results, as we all know, were not good. The Tennessee Department of Education estimated that instead of a normal summer learning loss, the state's students were likely to lose as much as a full year of instruction between when schools closed in March of 2020 and September of the following year.[1] Tennessee is likely to be the canary in the coal mine, and COVID-related learning losses are probably going to last for years.

So I've expanded my list of the questions I now know parents are asking (or should). There are, in fact, school secrets parents need to know. This book collects many of the often unwritten rules that can make a child's K–12 experience the best it can be. I figured that basing a book around the questions parents ask would be a good way to get them the answers they need.

For the answers to those questions, I often turned to the real experts, parents. I spoke with parents of kids who attended public schools, charter schools, private schools, and homeschools. Some were at the start of their schooling journey, with kids in early elementary school. Others had watched as their kids moved on to college and beyond. I am grateful beyond measure for their generosity and honesty in sharing their stories.

I'm also grateful to the teachers and school administrators who opened up about the things parents need to know but that schools don't always tell them. Sometimes, parents and schools find themselves on what feels like opposite sides of a chasm, speaking a different language. (Say, what *is* a "stanine," anyway?) So finding ways to bridge that divide is critical, and they helped me do that.

There's a lot of research in here as well. Education research studies are often almost impenetrable. ("Do I put my kid in kindergarten this year or not?") I've included links to the studies wherever I can so you can delve deeper if you feel a strong need. Or can't sleep some night.

And I do hope you'll find some humor here. Raising a kid in these times seems just unduly fraught. We have to take care of each other, and we have to take care of ourselves. Laughter helps.

Some of the tips I'll share with you will get you around the bureaucratic walls schools often put up. I'll show you how to

- decide whether to "redshirt" your kindergartner;
- figure out what your second grader should be learning in math, and how to talk with a teacher if you think that's not being taught;
- ask for a specific teacher for your child (even when the school tells you it isn't allowed);
- understand why you might want to reconsider buying tie shoes for your kindergartener;
- know which math classes will get your child into a selective college—and when you need to enroll your child in those classes (hint: it's earlier than you think);
- get to know the "secret gatekeeper" for college admissions—the high school counselor; and
- choose the school that's right for your child, whether it's an elementary school or a college.

In addition, I'll share tips on what you should—and shouldn't—do at home to help your child achieve, two phrases that will help you survive your child's middle school years, and suggestions on how to help with homework when your child knows more than you do. In all, there are 81 answers to questions that could help your child have success in school.

I won't promise you that every answer I give is right for your family—but these are the questions you need to think about at each stage of the school game. I hope they will be helpful as you navigate the challenging job of supporting your child as they move from preschool to postsecondary education.

And yes, I'll also let you in on why one secret to helping your child get the best possible education may just be playing in the band.

A word about how to read the book. Parents are mostly interested in dealing with the questions they are facing today, which is why it's organized so you don't have to wade through information on high school algebra when your child is just starting second grade. But there are a couple of chapters that are, by design, for everyone. Chapter 1 highlights some questions that parents are likely to ask again and again as their child moves through school. Chapter 8 gives information on homework including information on the brain research that can improve your child's learning. Chapter 9 is for parents who want to make a change in how their child's school operates, whether it's asking for a specific teacher for the next year or passing a state law.

Once you've read the questions that apply to your child today, you may well want to read ahead to see what's coming up. (This will be especially true for the people who always want to read the last chapter in a murder mystery so they know how things end.) If there's an upcoming question that seems particularly relevant, I've tried to point that out in the text.

And then there's Chapter 2, "When the Kitchen Table Becomes Your School Desk." It's the chapter I wish parents wouldn't have to read. But it's also the chapter that you may find is the most useful if your school closes down again. (And it very likely will.)

Finally, you'll note that the book uses pronouns, specifically the singular "they," in a way you're not used to seeing. When you write about kids, you write about individuals. And that has meant that over the years, I've tried to use a singular pronoun after "your child." It was sometimes a struggle.

In school, I was taught that "he" could be a generic singular, referring to either a boy or a girl. But I hated it even then and wanted no part of it here. Neither did I want to say "he or she" about 50 billion times throughout this manuscript. It goes without saying that I would never write s/he because, well, it's just ugly.

Over the years, I had mostly settled on an alternating he/she style that was both clunky and ultimately still somewhat confusing. ("Boys can have trouble with friends, too, you know," a mom wrote to me after reading an article on friendships that had used more "shes" than "hes.") I also wrote in the plural. ("Children can leave their book bags by the door.") None of these felt exactly right.

In 2020, I realized that the world had moved on and I had not. Somewhere in the 21st century, people had just settled on the notion that "they" could be a singular pronoun. As Benjamin Dreyer wrote in *Dreyer's English*, "The singular 'they' is not the wave of the future; it's the wave of the present."[2] And so that's what I'm using.

1

SIX BIG QUESTIONS
ALL PARENTS SHOULD ASK

*The most important people in a child's life are that child's parents
and teachers. That means parents and teachers are the most important
people in the world.*

—Fred Rogers

Being a parent means you are playing a constant game of catch-up. As
soon as you figure out how to kid-proof the house so your 18-month-
old doesn't stick their finger in the light socket, along come the terrible
twos. In late elementary school, just as you're feeling like you're doing
pretty well as a parent, puberty kicks in.

Helping kids move through school typically follows a similar pattern.
The things you will worry about when your child goes to kindergarten are,
by and large, not the same things you'll worry about in elementary school.
So this book is organized to highlight the most important questions you're
likely to ask for each level of schooling.

However, there are some bigger questions—things that parents return
to over and over as their child progresses through school. Here are six that
won't change as your child moves through school, although the *answers*
sometimes will. The issues that result in a kid missing school are very different for a kindergartener than for a high school senior.

1. HOW CAN I RAISE A KID WHO LOVES LEARNING?

What's the key to helping a child be successful in school? There's a good
case to be made for curiosity and an interest in learning. A child who
shows up at school wanting to learn—well, pretty much anything will find

a way. And while they're exploring their fascination for caterpillars or cars or cooking rice, they're pretty likely to be open to learning other things.

Children are naturally curious. As they learn more about their world, it's almost impossible to keep them from exploring, asking questions, and trying to figure things out. But somewhere along the line, that natural curiosity sometimes seems to disappear. What can parents do to keep their delight in learning alive?

Perhaps the best way to answer that question is to tell you about my sister's friend and her basement. My sister lived in an old house with a lower level that could only be called a "cellar"—it was dark and dingy. No one went down there if they didn't have to. One day she was commiserating with a friend who had a similar basement. "It's so gloomy we try not to keep anything down there," the friend said.

"Oh, except for the rocket room."

One of her sons was obsessed with rockets. He wanted to read about them. He wanted to build them. He wanted to test various rocket engines. And all that required plenty of open space. So in their dark and dingy lower level, the family carved out Steven's rocket room.

We've all known a child who becomes fixated on a subject. Often, it's dinosaurs. But it could be baseball statistics, horses, or possibly (even though you are hoping this is made up) slugs.

Not every child, you will be grateful to learn, delves as deeply into a subject as the rocket-room kid. But at one time or another, most kids become fascinated by a particular topic. The child often develops real expertise, with the ability to distinguish a sauropod from a theropod at a single glance. That in turn can give kids a big boost of confidence. It is, for example, very satisfying when the dinosaur devotee can recognize 250 species while Mom and Dad can identify at most 10.

Following an interest helps children develop a longer attention span, persistence, and a better ability to process information.[1] They'll ask questions and look for answers on their own. All those are helpful—and will work just as well when they're studying state capitals, long division, or Spanish vocabulary words.

Typically, these obsessions last for somewhere between six months and three years before petering out. But sometimes, as with the rocket-room kid, they linger. While they're in full swing, there are some things parents can do that will keep the child motivated . . . or squelch their interest.

Perhaps the most critical thing for parents to understand is that the interest is your child's, not yours. Parents can introduce their child to a sport they love or a hobby they enjoy. But that does not mean the child will love it as much as you do. In fact, parents who try to push a particular interest on their child are typically met with failure.

That means that allowing children to have some control over their own interest is a good way to keep them engaged. In one study, researchers followed middle school students who were just learning to play an instrument. One of the major predictors of the students who ended up developing a passion for the music was whether their parents gave them freedom to practice on their own schedule.[2]

As educational researcher Benjamin Bloom found when he analyzed highly talented individuals in many fields, parents play a critical role. Your job is primarily to provide "motivational support and encouragement."[3] Bloom suggested "playful learning" across a wide range of subjects while the child is young. Then as a particular interest develops, you can look for ways to support your child's desire to learn more.

Building a love of learning is one of the best gifts you can give your child, and the best way to do that is by building on your child's interests. When kids develop this love at an early age, it will carry them through the times when they have to learn more about a subject that might not fascinate them. They'll be able to take joy in learning something they never knew before.

Not every interest will last throughout your child's entire school career. But Steven, the rocket-room denizen, did in fact go on to earn a graduate degree in rocket science. Some young dinosaur fans do start to think of themselves as paleontologists. And some kids who start by picking out a tune on the piano end up giving recitals. Many more will understand that they are capable of learning, of persisting, and of mastering a subject.

And as adults, they'll be better able to adapt to a world and a workplace that change rapidly. A willingness to learn is required for every job.

Children have the potential to learn and do much more than most adults ever imagine. So look for those glimmers of interest and see how your child develops them.

Developing curiosity

Here are four ways parents can develop a child's natural curiosity:

1. Plant seeds and watch as they grow into flowers or tomatoes. Buy some yeast and try baking a loaf of bread, checking in to

see how the dough rises. Fill a small cup with water and put it in the freezer. Let the ice melt; then boil the water on the stove until it turns to steam.

2. Encourage your child to ask questions. When your child asks why, help them find the answer. Help them keep a "wonder journal," where they record the questions they want to learn more about. You can take the wonder journal to the library and check out books that will help them follow up. Or look for TV shows that help explain the questions they are pondering.

3. Pick a topic to learn about together. Read books, look online, do things together. Later, have "book talk" conversations. Ask your child to share important ideas in their own words. You can help your child build knowledge and develop a love of learning.

4. Promote active learning whenever you can. It's not always necessary for parents to build out a rocket room or to buy hundreds of dinosaur replicas, but both you and your child might enjoy it. You don't have to give an 8-year-old budding gastronome a rice cooker, but you'll probably reap some rewards at dinnertime. However, if you are very unlucky and find yourself creating a habitat for a family of slugs in your child's bedroom, well, you can only hope this will be a fairly short-lived obsession.

2. HOW CAN I HELP MY CHILD LEARN FROM FAILURE?

They didn't make the team. They didn't get cast in the role they wanted in the school play. They ran for student council president and another candidate won.

Sooner or later, even the luckiest and most gifted student is going to experience failure. For some, it provides motivation to work harder. But for others, the failure can seem insurmountable.

The reality is that sometimes the things students have to learn in school are just plain hard. And that probably means that your child will not master these skills on the first try. So parents need to help children see failure as an opportunity to learn.

Yet too many parents don't. And that, according to the founders of Harvard's Success–Failure Project (yes, there really is such a thing), has led to a generation of students who are "failure deprived."[4]

The story of basketball player Michael Jordan illustrates the ways failure can lead to ultimate success. He famously failed to make the varsity basketball team as a sophomore in high school, while his friend Leroy Smith did. Jordan was devastated. (The fact that Michael was 5′10″ at the time, while Leroy was 6′7″, seems not to have entered Jordan's mental calculations at all.)

By his junior year, Jordan had worked hard to improve his basketball skills. (He'd also grown 4 inches.) He made the varsity team that year and . . . well, you know the rest of the story. It was, Jordan said, the memory of that initial failure that kept him in the gym, even when he was tired and wanted to quit.

Many years later, when he was inducted into the NBA Hall of Fame, Jordan reflected on the impact of that early failure and the motivation it provided him. "I wanted to prove not just to Leroy Smith, not just to myself, but to the coach who picked Leroy over me, I wanted to make sure you understood, you made a mistake, dude."[5]

Jordan's may be among the most well-known failure-to-success stories, but it is hardly unique. Most of us have a story of how we overcame some challenge. So why do we, as parents, so often work hard to keep our kids from ever experiencing failure? We write the essay or do the science project. We fight with the teacher to change a report card grade. We yell at the referee who has the temerity to call a foul on our child.

And what's the result of trying to wrap kids in bubble wrap so they don't take a bump? Overprotective parenting never ends well. In the worst-case scenario, these hyperprotective parents may end up like actress Lori Loughlin, sentenced to a stretch in jail for her efforts to guarantee her kids a spot in a competitive college. (More on this in Question 5.)

But even when things don't go that far, the overprotective parenting keeps kids from learning some important lessons. So instead of protecting your child from failure, here are the things you can help them learn from it.

Failure doesn't have to be permanent. The most important lesson you need to teach your child is that their failure isn't permanent. If they didn't make the team, they can practice and try out again. If they got a bad grade on a math test, they can study and do better next time.

Try using the acronym FAIL: First Attempt in Learning. Whether your child is learning a new piece on the piano or starting to study long division, that first attempt is likely to be messy. That's when you say, "Remember, it's a First Attempt in Learning. Just keep at it."

Malcolm Gladwell argued that it takes roughly 10,000 hours of talent to achieve real mastery of any skill. There's been some disagreement about the exact number since he first wrote it in his book *Outliers*, but his basic point is still the same: Nobody's born an expert. It takes a lot of messy practice before you achieve anything like world-class skill in cognitively complex activities. And that means that there are a lot of hours of failure before things come together.[6]

There's more about the importance of seeing failure as a step in a process rather than the final destination in Question 73, Chapter 8.

You often learn the most from your failures. Think back to some of the big things you've learned in your life. Did you master it the first time? Or was your eventual success the product of some painstaking trials and errors?

When you fail at something, you can fail forward—moving closer to your goal even though you are not there yet. Helping children analyze what they've done right as well as what they've done wrong is a great way to help them become better problem solvers in the future. So when your child has experienced a failure, ask, "What did you learn from this? What would you do differently next time?"

Yet, as Sir Ken Robinson said in the TED Talk that has the highest viewership of all time, the only lesson we seem to teach children is that "mistakes are the worst thing you can make. [But] if you're not prepared to be wrong, you'll never come up with anything original."[7]

In their book *GIST: The Essence of Raising Life-Ready Kids*, authors Michael W. Anderson and Timothy D. Johanson compiled a long list of mistakes and curveballs you need to let your kid experience. Here are a few of them:

- not being invited to a birthday party;
- working hard on a paper and still getting a low grade;
- being told that a class or a camp is full;
- not making the varsity team; and
- coming in last at something.[8]

Changing paths. Of course, failure doesn't always lead to subsequent success in the same field. Sometimes, failure can serve as a springboard to finding a new path.

My daughter Sara also did not make a team (in this case soccer) her first year in high school. Like Michael Jordan, she was devastated. She'd played soccer for years and had many friends who were on the squad.

But instead of doubling down and working on her soccer skills, she decided to try something new. She signed up for the crew team (whose no-cut policy probably seemed pretty appealing). Now, she was not the rowing equivalent of Michael Jordan, but she was good enough and dedicated enough to make the varsity boat in high school. She even rowed for a year at Princeton.

A child who loves the theater may not end up acting onstage. They can design the lighting or the scenery. They can run the box office or develop the advertising campaign. Sometimes a failure does not lead to a completely different path, just a slight detour.

Resilience. Growing up involves uncertainty—will today's best friend still like you tomorrow? Will your family have to move for a new job? Will you lose a beloved pet to illness or old age? How kids adapt to that uncertainty is in part based on their resilience.

As defined by the American Psychological Association, *resilience* is the ability to adapt well to adversity, trauma, tragedy, threats, or even significant sources of stress. It's how your child can deal with difficult situations. When they know they have the skills and confidence to address and work through one problem, they are more likely to have the confidence to face the next tough challenge. The more kids bounce back on their own, the more they internalize the message that they are strong and capable.

"Those who see errors as opportunities to learn and try again are the people who will most quickly find new solutions. (This is how our children become resilient.) Those who freeze and panic when they make mistakes will find it much harder to adapt," said Madeline Levine in *Ready or Not: Preparing Our Kids to Thrive in an Uncertain and Rapidly Changing World.*[9]

How do parents do that? Levine advised, "The best way we can help our children welcome challenges is to encourage them to work just outside their comfort zone, stand by to lend a hand when needed, and model enthusiasm for challenging tasks."[10]

Learning how to win. Finally, failure can teach kids how to win. We try to encourage our kids to be gracious losers, and that's an important life skill. But it's also important to understand how to be a good winner.

If your child loses a race to a kid who's a jerk, they'll understand what *not* to do when the tables are turned. So when they complain about the opponent who bragged insufferably, just remind them that their turn is coming to show some grace in victory.

And here, the example of Leroy Smith might be instructive. He's the player who *made* the varsity team the year Michael Jordan got cut. And while we don't know a lot about how he acted toward his friend during that year, we get some idea from what happened years later. Apparently, he turned out to be a pretty gracious winner.

Because if you watch Michael's speech at the NBA Hall of Fame Awards ceremony, you'll see that Leroy Smith was also there.

He was there as Jordan's guest.

3. HOW MUCH TV AND SCREEN TIME IS TOO MUCH?

For years, parents and teachers both worried about whether school-age kids were spending too much time staring at a screen. Then came COVID-19, when everything from playdates to class time abruptly went virtual. Suddenly, 3 billion children around the world were confined to their homes, and nearly every school district in the United States stopped holding in-person classes.

Even before the pandemic, a study by Iowa State University researcher Douglas Gentile found, "Children now spend as much as 60 hours a week in front of some kind of screen and more than 40 percent of children ages 4–6 have a TV in their bedroom. A substantial majority of children 8 and older have a TV or video game console in their bedrooms."[11]

The American Academy of Pediatrics (AAP) used to suggest a flat-out ban on all screen time for the youngest children.[12] In 2020, they relaxed that position somewhat. They now say that for children 18–24 months old, video chatting can be a good way to build relationships with distant family or friends.

But for older children, a strict guideline makes no sense when that wouldn't even cover the time a child spends on second-grade reading, math, and science classes. Clearly, parents need new guidelines.

Experts now recommend that parents think not only about how *much* time children are spending in front of a screen, but what they're doing. Here are some tips:

- Staying in touch with friends and family is important for children. When they cannot see their friends at school or at the playground, technology is sometimes the best substitute.[13] Social media can also help families stay connected when it's not safe for them to be together in person. During the pandemic, grandparents shared story after story reading books with their grandchildren via FaceTime.

- For many children, online school was the only real learning opportunity available during the pandemic. When schools closed in March of 2020, many parents figured it would be a temporary solution. But spring stretched to summer and summer became fall, and still schools remained largely shut. It's now clear that families need a way for children to continue learning even when the school building is closed. The challenges of moving to a fully virtual classroom are explored in the next chapter.

- The more interactive online presence that today's kids are likely to carve out is different from watching a few hours of cartoons or another viewing of *Frozen*. Parents need to be more involved with what their child is doing and who they are interacting with. Luckily, many of the risks that parents worry about can be at least mitigated, if not eliminated, with some active parent involvement. This includes talking with kids about their online experiences. Who are they communicating with? How do they know them? Parents also need to be aware of the games that children play and play them together. (During the pandemic, many adults discovered that Animal Crossing was as soothing to a frazzled parent as it was to a 6-year-old.)

- It's still a good idea to limit TV time, and to keep TVs out of the bedroom. The Iowa State researchers who followed children for one or two years saw that having media (TV or video games) in the bedroom unsurprisingly increased their total screen time. That affected their grades, probably because third- through fifth-grade students who spent more time watching TV spent less time reading. Increased screen time was also linked to higher body mass index, physical aggression, and symptoms of video game addiction.[14] Look, it's hard to take a TV *out* of a child's room. But it's much easier never to put a set in there in the first place. And while you're at it, give cell phones a nighttime curfew by putting the charging station somewhere other than your child's room. Truth to tell, no good comes from anything that happens on the internet at 2:30 a.m.

- Learn how to set up internet controls—and use them. Give your kids a password to use the internet, but place time limits on when the password can be used. If you find that your tech-savvy kids have figured out how to disable these controls, let them use devices only in places where you can supervise.

- Watch how your kids behave after they have been online, watched TV, or played a video game. If their behavior is positive, they are using age-appropriate media (and yes, that means you have to check in regularly), and they are enjoying other nonscreen activities as well, you probably don't need to worry.
- Provide alternative ways to have fun. Purchase some board games. Get a deck of cards—children may be amazed to learn that people played solitaire long before there were cell phones! Visit the library regularly.
- Be a good role model yourself. You can't expect kids to turn off the TV if you have it on as wallpaper all day. And you can't ask them to give up their phones if you never take your nose out of your email and social media accounts. When the Pew Research Center surveyed parents and teens about technology use, more than one third of parents (36%) said they spent too much time looking at their screens. But 51% of teens felt that parents were sometimes or often distracted when they were trying to talk to them, so parents may not even be aware of how their teens feel.[15]

4. WHAT'S THE BEST WAY TO DEVELOP A STRONG PARTNERSHIP WITH THE SCHOOL?

"When parents are involved in their children's education at home, they do better in school. And when parents are involved in school, children go farther in school—and the schools they go to are better." That was the conclusion reached by researchers Anne Henderson and Nancy Berla in 1994.[16] Since then, additional research has only confirmed their statement.

Starting as early as preschool,[17] research clearly shows when parents are more involved in their child's education, the student will have

- higher grades and test scores;
- improved reading scores;
- better and more regular school attendance; and
- a positive attitude and more appropriate behavior.

So how can parents develop a strong partnership with their child's school?

Build a relationship with the teachers and the school. Right from the start, get to know your child's teachers. This is as important in high school as it is in first grade. Take younger children to school on the first day and, if you can, walk them to their classroom. And when your child reaches upper elementary school and tells you in no uncertain terms to stay away on the first day, reach out anyway.

Write a letter to your child's teachers. Let them know you want to work together to improve your child's education. Give them information on the best time and the best way to contact you—email? Text? Phone call?

Gather as much information as you can. You'll also want to find out as much as you can about your child's school. From the school calendar (write down the dates of the teacher workdays now so you aren't surprised later) to the lunch menu, you can probably find the answers to many of your questions on the school website. Other vital information will come in your child's backpack, so be sure you clean it out and read the brightly colored flyers that have been stuffed in the bottom.

Get to know other parents, who may clue you in on something that you need to know. In Sara's elementary school, parents were invited to eat a Thanksgiving lunch in the cafeteria a week before Thanksgiving. I figured it was optional and nearly passed it up. Fortunately, my friend Cynthia called me from the school. "This is a big deal," she said. "Get over here."

Early in the school year, you'll probably receive an invitation to Back to School Night. It's a valuable way to build a stronger relationship with your child's teachers. You won't be able to discuss specific issues like your child's current worries about their math grade, but once you and the teacher have seen each other and exchanged a few words, you'll find it's easier to reach out with questions or comments later.

Attend parent–teacher conferences. The best time and place to have a one-on-one conversation about your child is at parent–teacher conferences. Typically held twice a year, these meetings offer a block of time for sharing ideas and addressing issues. If your school schedules conferences during your regular work hours, ask if there's another time you and the teacher could meet. Here are some issues you may want to raise:

- Attendance. Kids can't learn if they aren't in school. As early as kindergarten, school attendance matters. If your child is not attending school regularly, talk about ways to address whatever issues are keeping them at home.
- Academics. What should your child know and be able to do by the end of this school year? Does the teacher think your child is on track to achieve those standards? If not, how can you work at home to support their progress?

- Attitude. How does your child behave in class? How do they get along with other students?

You may want to share other information about your child. If there is a challenging situation at home, it may be affecting your child's work and behavior at school. The teacher will be better able to address it if you share that information.

Find a way to help. Teaching is a hard job, and there's never enough time for one person to do it all. If you have time to volunteer in the classroom, you can provide an extra set of hands for a busy teacher. You could read to a child or listen to a child read to you. You could quiz a child on math facts. If you have a special skill (such as speaking a second language), you can support the learning not just of your own child but of every student at the school. If you don't have time to volunteer regularly, make yourself available for one-time activities such as Career Day.

You'll want to join your school's parent–teacher association. These dedicated parent volunteers work together on everything from the book fair to the all-night graduation party. When every parent spends a little time working for the school, the results can be dramatic. Consider serving on a school or district advisory group. This may be a way to share your professional expertise in shaping policy for your school district. You also bring a parent's voice to those who are making policy decisions. Many districts have advisory groups on issues ranging from serving students with disabilities to selecting math textbooks, so there is likely to be a spot for you.

Finally, be sure you talk with your child every day about school. If you've met your child's teacher and visited the classroom, you'll be able to ask questions that go beyond just, "How was school today?" You can ask about the class pet or the book the teacher is reading aloud. Ask what your child is most looking forward to tomorrow or what they did at recess. And you can always ask your child to tell you something they learned today.

You could ask your middle or high school student to tell you about the most interesting thing they learned at school, or something they learned that they think they might use again. You could also ask them to teach you something they think you don't know. Ask what they think makes a good teacher and whether any of their current teachers meet those standards. Or ask them if there's a class they'd like to take next semester or next year.

Or you could learn from Isidor Rabi, who won the Nobel Prize in Physics. Rabi was once asked why he became a scientist. He answered: "My mother made me a scientist without ever knowing it. Every other child would come back from school and be asked, 'What did you learn today?' But my mother used to say, 'Izzy, did you ask a good question today?' That made the difference. Asking good questions made me into a scientist."[18] Every now and then, ask your child, "Tell me a good question you asked today." You could be raising a scientist.

5. HOW MUCH PARENT INVOLVEMENT IS TOO MUCH?

As an elected official, I was sometimes called on to judge elementary school science fairs. It was always fun to see the experiments kids had designed to answer some question that might have been puzzling them. What *does* happen when a volcano erupts? Can plants live without light?

Of course, there were also some projects that you were *pretty sure* had not been completed by the child whose name was on the entry label. That was the case of the scale model of a nuclear reactor. Which was purportedly constructed by a first grader.

As far back as 1990, researchers Foster Cline and Jim Fay coined the term *helicopter parent* to label the parents who hover over their child and their child's teacher. Today, helicopter parents have been eclipsed by "snowplow" parents (sometimes called *bulldozer* parents). They don't just hover. They directly intervene and bulldoze any obstacles out of their child's way.

These parents don't just supervise homework—they write the paper. They don't just get to know the child's teacher—they come in and argue every time their child earns anything less than an A.

The most infamous helicopter parents were those caught up in the scandal that came to be known as Varsity Blues. More than 50 parents with engaged in a comprehensive fraud designed to get their children into prestigious colleges. They paid six-figure bribes to college coaches to get their children admitted as recruited athletes. They paid off college testing proctors so someone else could take their child's college admissions test.

And, of course, most of them ended up being convicted of a crime, several doing at least some time in prison. Those who eventually pled guilty included actresses Felicity Huffman and Lori Loughlin, wealthy business owners like Robert Flaxman and Douglas Hodge. There was even the author of a book on parenting, Jane Buckingham, on the list.

But they were not the first parents who were a little *too* involved with their child's education. Mary Pinkney Hardy MacArthur, mother of General George MacArthur, apparently moved to West Point when her son enrolled there. She lived nearby and supervised everything he did—sometimes through binoculars—to ensure he graduated first in his class. Later, she even wrote to Army Chief of Staff John Pershing asking him to "give my boy his well earned promotion."[19] (If you don't think that's at least a little creepy, this might not be the book for you.)

Helicopter parenting doesn't end up having the desired result. Indiana University psychologist Chris Meno has seen the unfortunate results of that overinvolvement. "When children aren't given the space to struggle through things on their own, they don't learn to problem-solve very well. They don't learn to be confident in their own abilities, and it can affect their self-esteem. The other problem with never having to struggle is that you never experience failure and can develop an overwhelming fear of failure and of disappointing others. Both the low self-confidence and the fear of failure can lead to depression or anxiety."[20]

Do teachers know what's going on? Of course. But there isn't always a lot they can do. As Julie Lythcott-Haims, who spent more than a decade as the freshman dean at Stanford, observed, "[I]t turns out it's very hard for all but the most seasoned of teachers to stand up to a well-heeled parent wielding a glue gun."[21]

Washington Post education columnist Jay Mathews shared a cautionary tale. "My favorite story comes from an admissions dean at Princeton who, when he inspected the little box on an application that certifies everything the applicant has written is the truth, found that the student's mother had signed it."[22]

How can you tell if you're a helicopter parent? If you use the first-person *plural* when discussing your child's school projects (as in, "We have that diorama to finish this weekend"), you're a helicopter parent. If you make an average of three extra school trips each week to drop off things your child forgot, you're a helicopter parent with bulldozer tendencies. And if your child's kindergarten science project was a model nuclear reactor (I would not have believed it if I hadn't seen it myself), you've crossed into the realm of the bulldozer parent.

Helicopter parenting is not good for you, and it's certainly not good for your kid. So how do you break this pattern?

- Watch your language. It's the first signal that you're too involved. If you find yourself talking about "our" book report, it's time to let it become *theirs* again. And "we" did not get into the gifted program—your child did.
- Resign from the rescue squad. A kid who puts off doing a report until the night before may just have to suffer the consequences of

a late night and a bad grade. Trust me, this will not keep that child out of college. But when kids never understand that they have to take responsibility for their own work, they could wind up living in the basement forever. "The parents who are the most helpful are the ones who call and say, 'He's getting off track. What can we do together to get him back headed in the right direction?'" said former Fairfax County (Virginia) public school teacher Joan Reynolds.

- Don't always blame the teacher. "Don't look on teachers as the enemy," Reynolds pleaded. "We honestly don't want to flunk every kid. But we do want them to develop the wherewithal so they can stand on their own when they get to college."
- De-escalate. There may be a time during your child's school career when you have to do battle with the school. But a C on a social studies quiz in the fourth grade is not that time. Stay out of fighting over your child's grade, the school's discipline policies, and especially your child's spot on an athletic team. When your child faces a problem, make time to talk about it—and then ask, "Well, what do you think might work?"
- Respect teachers. Make appointments. Use email. Don't drop in unannounced and insist that the teacher deal with your concern immediately. One music teacher reported that a parent walked by his classroom every time her child was in the class "just to see for myself whether she is happy." Every. Single. Time.
- Let your child face the consequences. Sooner or later, your child is going to have to learn to take responsibility for their own life. So unless you're planning to go on their first job interview, give your child practice in handling things. (There is no such thing as "Take Your Parents to Work Day.") *Forbes* noted that today's parents seem comfortable submitting resumes, attending interviews, and even intervening in a work-related disciplinary issue.[23] Reynolds recalled the time when a student turned in her paper after the end of school, having missed school to write it (a clear violation of Reynolds's rule). "I reminded her of the rule and told her I would not accept the paper." The parents were, at first, stunned. They begged. They pleaded. They told Reynolds their daughter would never get into college, let alone achieve her dream of going to med school. Reynolds held firm and asked the parents to trust her judgment. With some trepidation, they agreed. "Today, she *is* a doctor—a doctor who has a very healthy respect for deadlines," Reynolds noted.

6. DOES ATTENDANCE REALLY MATTER?

"Success," Woody Allen once said, "is 20% timing and 80% just showing up." But when your middle schooler has worked late on a big project and wants to sleep in . . . or the star of the spring musical wants to be rested for the big performance at night . . . you may find yourself wondering whether it's really that important to get to school.

The answer is simple and clear. Yes. Attendance matters. A lot.

Research clearly shows a strong link between student achievement and student attendance. Students who miss school fall behind. This leads to a downward spiral—the student doesn't understand the material, gets frustrated, skips again.

The negative impact of missing school starts early. A comprehensive study done by Attendance Works, a program of the National Center for Children in Poverty, found that children who were "chronic absentees" in kindergarten still had the lowest performance in reading and math *in the fifth grade*. The study defined *chronic absentees* as students who missed 10% of school days per year—roughly 18 days in a 180-day school year. But that means that children who have missed just 2 days a month can fall into this category and suffer the impact on their learning.[24]

The Baltimore City Schools looked at the impact of missing too much school for students in the middle grades. By sixth grade, absenteeism was a signal that the student would fail to graduate from high school. And by ninth grade, students who missed 20 days of school (again, roughly 2 days per month) were more likely to fail their courses and not graduate.[25]

There are other reasons parents should worry if their child isn't in school. Chronic absenteeism also is a risk factor for many out-of-school problems, including drug use, delinquency, adult criminality, suicide attempts, and employment problems.[26] And while turning school problems over to law enforcement is a good way to make them even bigger problems, you should be aware that truancy laws are on the books in many states.

So what can you do to make sure your child attends school regularly? Here are some tips from parents:

- Be consistent. Make sure your child knows you aren't going to give them an easy excuse on the day they want to sleep in or delay taking their chemistry test.
- Be responsible yourself. Sometimes, kids are forced to miss school because their parents have no backup childcare.

- If missing school is a new behavior, there may be a problem you need to address. Talk with your child to find out why they don't want to go to school. Is someone bullying them? Are they failing a class? You can't solve a problem if you don't know what's going on.
- Don't make it too fun to stay home. If they are too sick to go to school, they're too sick to watch TV, go on the computer, text message friends, or play video games.

2

WHEN THE KITCHEN TABLE
BECOMES YOUR SCHOOL DESK

*Been homeschooling a 6-year-old and 8-year-old for one hour and
11 minutes. Teachers deserve to make a billion dollars a year. Or
a week.*

—Shonda Rhimes

There's a commercial for an office supply store that always strikes a chord with parents. It typically airs in late summer as back-to-school shopping gets in full swing. A father pushes a cart through the store, happily piling notebooks, pens, and other supplies into his cart. Two children trudge wordlessly behind. As the father continues to dance down the aisles, the soundtrack plays the Andy Williams Christmas hit "It's the Most Wonderful Time of the Year."

The message here is not hard to discern: Parents depend on schools for many reasons. But not the least of them is that schools give children a place to go five days a week for nine months a year.

When school is closed for even a day, it can cause major upheavals in family schedules. But when schools closed in the spring of 2020 as part of the nationwide response to the coronavirus, the school year effectively ended for more than 50 million U.S. students.

Virtually overnight, schools and families had to shift from the traditional teacher-in-classroom model of learning to the kids-at-home-on-the-couch model. Teachers had to create entirely new lesson plans that would work on video. They had to supervise online chat functions that could be easily hijacked by teens with tech skills far better than their own. They had to figure out how to provide one-on-one help to students they might not have heard from in more than a month.

Meanwhile, parents had to figure out how to set up a classroom in their living room, locate a log-in name and password that might have been sent to them at the beginning of the year (and might be different for every class), and plan a schedule that would include some online learning and some time when their children would be working independently at home. (Based on everything we now know, we should perhaps put both "working" and "independently" in quotation marks.)

The logistical challenges—even for families with devices and connectivity—were daunting. Who got access to the computer when? What took priority if Mom had a Zoom call at 10:00 and that was the time when Mrs. Jackson was teaching a math lesson? Those challenges didn't begin to touch on the *learning* that was supposed to be taking place, with parents spending hours on Google figuring out how to impart at least some information about everything from state capitals to solving for x.

Many conversations with both parents and teachers confirm that results were . . . uneven. Teachers were frustrated when failing technology interrupted their carefully constructed lessons. Kids were frustrated because they couldn't see their friends. Parents were just frustrated.

For families without access to computers or tablets and high-speed internet, the adjustments weren't just fodder for Shonda Rhimes–like humor. They knew that their children were missing out on valuable learning. Many worked hard to get their children online. Albert Pollard, a former seatmate in the General Assembly, noted that in the rural area of Virginia where he lives, "local radio is advertising which libraries and community colleges are closed but still have their Wi-Fi on and accessible from the parking lot." We in Fairfax County initially found that story pretty unbelievable. Then people ventured out near our own public libraries, closed for the pandemic. The parking lot was full of cars with families trying to help children do their school assignments. Yes, Fairfax County had broadband. But it did these families no good if they couldn't afford it.

As the school year straggled to a close, there seemed to be consensus on only one thing: This was no way to educate our children. But when fall arrived, kids were still learning online. And my dreadful prediction is that spring 2021 will not be the last time we face major school closures. Robin Lake, director of the Center on Reinventing Public Education at the University of Washington, agreed. "Start planning for the next forced school closure. It will come. And next time, schools and districts will need to act quickly, not dither for months."[1]

Karen Hawley Miles, from the national research organization Education Resource Strategies, agreed as well. She said, in fact, that schools will need a "close fast, open slow" approach. That will mean that parents get even less lead time to prepare for a school closure . . . and that reopening plans may take even longer.[2]

So, sadly, let's assume that school closures are going to be part of the new normal. Here's where your attitude will play a huge role in your child's ultimate success in school.

Parent Stacey Finkel, who shepherded two adolescent boys through the first round of COVID closures in Arlington, Virginia, only to face an uncertain second year of the same, said that part of her role is to give her boys an optimistic view. "I am getting into a more positive head space," she said a few weeks before the school year was slated to start. "I think for myself, for my community, for my family, this is how it's going to be. We all have to embrace it and understand its limitations. And having me present a negative posture about it does not benefit my kids.

"We are going to fail at some pieces of this. So we [schools, parents, and students] have to cut each other a break. Our kids are going to be heading into schooling and education that no one has ever seen before, ever. We have to support our community, our teachers, and the kids."

Here are some questions parents need to ask about learning at home, your role, and how best to help your kid.

7. SO MUCH OF ONLINE LEARNING SEEMS TO RELY ON PARENTS. HOW CAN I GET MYSELF IN THE HOME-LEARNING MINDSET?

First, take a deep breath. You've done more teaching than you probably realize. If your child was not born already knowing how to walk and eat with utensils and speak in complete sentences, you are very likely the teacher who imparted that knowledge.

Keith Butcher, clinical assistant professor of school leadership at the University of Houston, offered some reassurance to parents who are taking their first crack at home instruction. "I have always believed that every parent was their child's first and only life-long teacher. So, being a teacher for your child is natural; it's something you do every day. The only thing different is the context," he said.[3]

But boy, did the context change in the spring of 2020. This chapter is based on interviews with several parents of kids ranging in age from kindergarten through high school. Their experiences, all different, point to what enormous challenges they faced.

Until schools closed in 2020, Lindsay and Jonathon Dworkin's second-grade daughter Riley had loved everything about her school in Montgomery County, Maryland. "Riley was just made for school," Lindsay said. "She loves the structure, the organization, the pace, the socializing with peers. But she also respects the authority of the teacher. School gives her a purpose and a sense of belonging."

For the first two weeks, the Dworkins, like many other parents, thought that school closure might be like an extended series of snow days. So they dug through Riley's backpack to find any unfinished worksheets that they could have her complete.

But when it became clear that they were going to be at home for the long haul, they turned to family for help. Lindsay's mom and her sister, a certified teacher, both helped map out some learning activities for Riley. Her mom ordered books that she and Riley could read together on the regular FaceTime calls she set up. Those hours were not only precious for Riley—they were lifesavers for Lindsay and Jonathon. "We knew she was going to be engaged in a learning activity and happy, and that meant we could grab an hour to do our own work."

Renee and Justin Lang, whose daughter Evelyn was in kindergarten in Fairfax County, Virginia, went online to find help and support as the school closure stretched on and on. "Facebook groups of parents sprang up. We turned to them for a reminder that we were really not in this alone," Renee said. The Langs also found that Evelyn's adjustment to home learning would be much easier if they reached out to her teacher for advice.

"Early on, we realized that Evelyn was really not paying attention to the on-screen class. I immediately wrote to the teacher and said that we needed help. Evelyn is really social and she missed that interaction. I asked, 'Can we set up a time with you to just do that?' So every Monday, Evelyn and her teacher would have lunch together." That one-on-one time helped Evelyn feel less isolated and helped her parents stay connected with what she was supposed to be learning.

Your attitude matters. If you can approach at-home learning with the same attitude as when you were teaching your child to walk or ride a bike, you'll be less stressed. And so will your child. So reach out to other parents, perhaps through social media. And remember that sites like Instagram need to be taken with a very, very large grain of salt. You can be sure the other children in your child's third-grade class were not baking bread every day. And their kids are no better at long division than yours.

8. HOW DO I SET UP
A SCHEDULE FOR AT-HOME LEARNING?

One of the things kids come to rely on most is the *structure* of a school day. They know what's expected of them, and they know when certain things, whether it's a reading group or lunch, will take place. Families that were successful in navigating home learning found that they also had to create a schedule.

In some cases, the school made that easy. Paige Kowalski, whose seventh-grade and 10th-grade sons attended the same Washington, DC, charter school, said the school made scheduling a priority. "Every Sunday night we received an email that laid out, hour by hour, each kid's schedule for every day of the week." Some of the classes, like Mandarin, were live. Other scheduled times told students what they should do offline (read this assignment or work these math problems). "I was stunned, frankly, by how seamless the school made it for us."

Many other parents did not have as much detailed scheduling from the school, so they often had to create their own schedule. "Riley's online classes were always in the morning, so we created rules for mornings in our house. We got up. We had breakfast. We got dressed for school," Lindsay Dworkin said.

Some schools, including Fairfax County, Virginia, had a particularly rough transition to remote learning. Parents in Fairfax faced particular challenges in creating some semblance of a regular school day. Renee Lang noted that although she is definitely not one of those "Pinterest moms who color codes the schedule right down to the lunch break," she and Justin found that Evelyn "just did better when we had some structure." So as they move into a second year of at-home learning, that's what they plan to implement.

As you set up your schedule, be aware of how short the learning blocks are likely to be. The Illinois State Board of Education issued a comprehensive guide to providing remote learning when schools were closed. Note that these guidelines reflect the limited amount of time parents can expect children to engage in direct learning when schools are closed.

Andrew Ellingsen, who teaches music and serves as an instructional coach for teachers across all elementary grades in Decorah, Iowa, offered this observation about kids and attention spans: "Kids can focus on a single activity for as many minutes as they are years old." In pre-K and kindergarten, that means kids have a sustained attention span of likely only 5 minutes. And one father who lived through three months of at-home learning with a kindergartener said, "Five minutes is probably generous."

The Langs found that the best way to get their daughter to work on class assignments was to "make it a game and work on it in little spurts." That's good advice for older kids as well. Even a high school student will need to take a break from a concentrated reading or writing assignment every 15 minutes or so. That doesn't mean they have to stop doing math and start reading a novel. But adult productivity gurus advise office workers to take a 5- or 6-minute break every 25 minutes or so. That advice is just as important for students learning at home.

Remember that your child will be learning even in nonschool situations. Many of the things you will do with your family will provide natural learning opportunities. Kids who never understood fractions suddenly figure them out when they are in the process of doubling a batch of cookies.

Table 2.1.   One State's Guidelines for At-Home Learning

Grade Level	Minimum	Maximum	Recommended Length of Sustained Attention
PreK	20 minutes/day	60 minutes/day	3–5 minutes
K	30 minutes/day	90 minutes/day	3–5 minutes
1–2	45 minutes/day	90 minutes/day	5–10 minutes
3–5	60 minutes/day	120 minutes/day	10–15 minutes
6–8	Class: 15 minutes/day Total: 90 minutes/day	Class: 30 minutes/day Total: 180 minutes/day	1 subject area or class
9–12	Class: 20 minutes/day Total: 120 minutes/day	Class: 45 minutes/day Total: 270 minutes/day	1 subject or class

Illinois State Board of Education. (2020, March 27). *Remote learning recommendations during CO-VID-19 emergency*, p. 17. Retrieved from https://www.isbe.net/Documents/RL-Recommendations-3-27-20.pdf

For parents who working remotely, these recommendations point to another very real challenge: How do you supervise your child's work while also trying to do your own? Because the reality is that a 5-year-old cannot be expected to do much online learning without a parent sitting right beside them.

In some families, the decision about which parent provided that close-up instructional support was easier. If one parent had their hours cut or had been furloughed, then that was the parent who took over more of the home learning. But if both parents were trying to keep their employers and clients happy, then compromises were obviously called for.

Parents typically took turns, with one doing office work starting early in the morning and the other extending the office day later into the evening. But there's no question it was hard on everyone.

Sharing devices also was a challenge. Imagine a home with one computer on a day when Kid 1 has a reading class at 9:30, Kid 2 has a math class that starts at 9:45, and you have a work-related Zoom call that starts at 10:00. There's no way to make sure everyone gets online at the appointed time, so you might have to ask the school if they could provide an additional device for your child. Otherwise, you just have to let the teachers know that you child will need access to the class at a different time. (This is called *asynchronous* instruction.)

9. WHAT OTHER LOGISTICS ARE INVOLVED IN DOING SCHOOL AT HOME?

Scheduling, and scheduling access to devices, will be just one part of the logistical challenges faced by families doing remote learning. There are plenty of others.

There needs to be a designated spot for the multiple online connections that are likely to take place throughout the day. Children will be online with classmates and teachers. Parents will likely be in at least one work-related meeting a day. And since most of us do not live in homes that include multiple Zoom-ready sites, you need a quiet spot that can become your "studio." It doesn't have to be fancy, but it should be quiet and have good light.

Paige Kowalski found that designating a specific spot for at-home learning was important for her seventh grader. "Being set up for school is not the same as being set up for homework. I learned that my seventh grader cannot do classes on his bed. He has to be at the dining room table."

If kids do their schoolwork everywhere in the house, then you'll spend half your time searching for the orange crayon or the 12″ ruler they need for a project. You do not need an Instagram-ready learning corner—the kitchen table can work just fine. But a regular study spot will help your child settle into a learning mindset, so make sure it is as free of distractions as possible.

Whenever possible, let kids have a say in when and how they want to do their schoolwork. It's a good way for them to take responsibility for their learning as well as to help them think about *how* they learn best. (And remember the research from Question 1, that allowing children to have some control over their own interest is a good way to keep them engaged.) A child who figures out that they can do better in math if they tackle it first thing in the morning will have learned something that will help them do better in college and in the workforce.

If that weren't complicated enough, sadly, some schools may insist that parents police what their kids wear. They may set dress codes for online classes. (One can only assume that they must be clueless about what many of their own teachers are wearing, at least on the body parts that are out of camera range.[4])

Not that every teacher *cares* if kids come to school in pajamas, of course. Baltimore kindergarten teacher Lindsay Arnold, for example, tweeted, "I don't care if my students show up in pajamas to school, and I most certainly do not care if they show up in pajamas while learning from their home." But if it's an issue with your school, your child can join the ranks of other American workers who look professional from the waist up.

10. HOW CAN PARENTS HELP FILL THE TIME PRODUCTIVELY WHEN STUDENTS ARE NOT IN FORMAL, TEACHER-DIRECTED LEARNING ACTIVITIES?

Even if your technology and your online connection with the school are operating perfectly, the reality is that this type of learning will occupy your kids for only a few hours a day. When states issued their guidance for remote learning, nearly every state limited the home "school day" to no more than 3 hours even for high school students.

Clearly, a parent could not rely on a child's sustained attention to get them through a full workday. Or even a single Zoom meeting.

What to do to fill the additional hours? Try to allow some time each day for your children to go outdoors to enjoy the fresh air. Obviously, parents need to protect their children during these trips, maintaining social distance or following rules about where it's safe to play. Outdoor time can also provide valuable science lessons. Lynn Mitchell of Staunton, Virginia, homeschooled her two children for a total of 16 years. She often used the outdoors for hands-on activities. "We might go down to the pond to get guppies. Or we'd collect leaves and turn them into an art project."

If your family has not scheduled a regular DEAR time (Drop Everything and Read), being quarantined at home is a great time to borrow this popular elementary school practice. Or assemble art supplies and let your child draw or paint or color. Have them write an old-fashioned letter to a friend or family member. Your child will feel more connected and will also have a chance to practice communication skills.

Crafts and hobbies are also lifesavers. "We did crafts," Renee Lang said. Since their quarantine experience began just before St. Patrick's Day, "we had a lot of shamrocks. A lot of shamrocks."

Observe weekends. When there are no outside activities to define your day, it's easy to feel like every day is the same as every other. But weekends are important. Give everyone in your family a chance to relax and do something different.

If possible, allow time for your child to pursue some independent learning—they may not read Shakespeare, but they might find out more about beetles. Paige Kowalski's older son loved having extra time after he'd finished his schoolwork. He worked on learning how to code. He taught himself to play the piano.

But other kids didn't do as well with a lot of unstructured time. Most parents just hoped to get through a day without having to resort to the 387th replay of *Frozen II*. As one mom told me, "There was a lot of screen time. There's still a lot of screen time. And I have to admit that sometimes, the screen was a babysitter."

Finally, don't panic if your children sometimes tell you they are bored. Lin-Manuel Miranda, creator of the musical *Hamilton*, reflected on the benefits of a childhood that included his share of boring hours. "Time alone is the gift of self-entertainment—and that is the font of creativity. Because there is nothing better to spur creativity than a blank page or an empty bedroom."[5]

OK, your kid may not grow up to write a sensational Broadway musical that captivates the world. But having an empty hour or two to fill will prepare a child for the boring job they will inevitably have at least once in their life. It will also help them learn that they can make something happen without relying on others. As Pamela Paul wrote in *The New York Times*, "Boredom leads to flights of fancy. But ultimately, to self-discipline. To resourcefulness."[6]

11. WHAT IF WE DON'T HAVE
THE TECHNOLOGY TO DO ONLINE LEARNING?

Computers are expensive, and internet connectivity is not always available. In the 2020 closures, schools learned that they need to provide computers to every student, just as they provide textbooks.

Schools tried (not always successfully) to distribute devices and hotspots during the spring of 2020. The organization Future Ready Schools found that 83% of member districts had made efforts to equip every student with a computer and internet access, but across the country, many children were not online.

Some schools loaned out classroom computers. Others turned to nonprofit organizations that could provide gently used and refurbished computers for children who need them. But many students never had a computer or other device and so were completely shut out of online learning once schools closed.

The Alliance for Excellent Education found that in the summer of 2020, after schools had been operating only in a virtual environment for four months, nearly 17 million students nationally lacked devices or the high-speed internet access needed to fully participate in online learning from home. That number included:

- 34% of American Indian/Alaska Native households having no high-speed internet access at home, and almost 16% with no computer;
- 36% of Americans living in rural areas of the United States lacking high-speed home internet, and 14% without a computer;
- 31% of Latino families without high-speed home internet, and 17% not having a computer;
- nearly 31% of Black households without high-speed home internet and 17% with no computer; and
- 5% of households making less than $25,000 annually with no high-speed home internet, and nearly 29% without a computer.[7]

Students need access to high-speed internet in order to do most online learning. A study by Common Sense Media found that 15–16 million K–12 public school students and 300,000–400,000 K–12 teachers, roughly 10% of all public school teachers, live in households without an internet connection or device adequate for remote learning.[8]

If you have a device but no high-speed internet, your family may be able to take advantage of the Federal Communications Commission's (FCC) Lifeline program for low-income families. It provides a $9.25 monthly subsidy for wireless or landline telephone service or broadband or bundled service. You can learn more at https://www.fcc.gov/general/lifeline-program-low-income-consumers. Or check with the internet service provider in your area. Many offered free or low-cost internet access during the time schools were closed.

Do not hide the fact that you need help to ensure your child will go online. Tell your child's teacher that you need a computer, an internet connection, or both. Ask for advice and help so your family can provide your children with the technology they need. If the school cannot provide these vital learning tools, they may be able to connect you with an organization that can help.

Organizations providing computers to low-income families

In addition to these largely national organizations, there are many local organizations that may be able to help you get the devices and connectivity your family needs.

PCs for People (https://www.pcsforpeople.org/) recycles donated computers to low-income families, those either with an income below the 200% poverty level or currently enrolled in an income-based government assistance program. Documentation is required.

The On It Foundation (http://theonitfoundation.org/) provides free donated computers to at-risk youth and families in need. K–12 students in a public school and on the free or reduced lunch program can qualify. Parents must submit a letter explaining their specific need and how the computer could benefit the child.

Computer Technology Assistance Corps (CTAC) (https://ctac-nh.org/node/12) refurbishes donated computers and then resells them at very low cost. Applicants must be receiving some sort of state or federal assistance, including free or reduced-price lunch.

If you live in southern California, you might check with Komputers 4 R Kids (http://www.komputers4rkids.com/). The organization provides qualifying students with a desktop computer bundle with a monitor, keyboard, mouse, and PC. An application is required.

---

12. WE HAVE BEEN SCHOOLING AT HOME AND MY CHILD IS CLEARLY STRUGGLING. WHAT DO I DO?

Learning at home proved to be a challenge for many students. But for some, especially those who were already behind their classmates or who had special education needs, the challenges became almost insurmountable obstacles.

The research organization NWEA estimated that all students were likely to return to school with some learning loss. But the kids who were already struggling and behind when schools went virtual might end up one or even two years behind their peers.

There are some things you can do. First, encourage your child to take part in learning activities that aren't specifically school related. Read books together, and encourage them to read alone. Reading is a skill that gets better with practice.

There are a number of online apps that can also teach and reinforce school content. Ask the teacher for recommendations, or check out the list at the end of this chapter.

Ask the school if they plan to provide tutoring for students who have fallen behind. There is considerable evidence that one-on-one tutoring can close learning gaps.[9]

Stacey Finkel said she learned an important lesson from a teacher friend: Speak up. "Students, teachers, and parents all need to articulate what they need. They may not even *know* what that is, so we will have to help. I'm going to ask my son, 'Do you need a brain break? Do you need to eat more? Do you need a standing appointment with your counselor or case manager?'"

Parents should speak up as well. If you're having trouble helping your child with online learning, ask whether the school has scheduled any training programs for parents. In San Antonio, Texas, the school district started with a few parent offerings but continued to expand as parents asked for more help.

13. NOW THAT I HAVE TAUGHT MY CHILD AT HOME, I'M WONDERING ABOUT CONTINUING TO HOMESCHOOL. WHAT SHOULD I THINK ABOUT BEFORE I MAKE THAT DECISION?

Helping children learn at home was a huge adjustment for most families. Many couldn't wait until their kids went back to the classroom and life got back to normal.

But for other parents, homeschooling began to look like a realistic alternative. When RealClear Opinion Research asked parents whether they were likely to continue homeschooling once the lockdowns were over, a surprising number said yes. Four in 10 parents (40.8%) said they'd consider homeschooling, a neighborhood co-op, or a virtual school, while 31.1% said they were less likely to do so. More Democrats (45.7%) than Republicans (42.3%) expressed an interest. More Black parents (50.4%) and Asian Americans (53.8%) said they'd consider homeschooling than white parents (36.3%) or Latino parents (38.2%).[10]

Could homeschooling be a more permanent choice for your family? Lynn Mitchell has thought a lot about the considerations for parents. "There's a big difference between schooling at home, which these families have been doing, and homeschooling," she said. "When you are homeschooling, you're all in, 24–7. You are not waiting for a pandemic to pass. So your first big job is to decide whether that's what you really want.

"Make an honest assessment of how your homeschooling experience has gone," she advised. "Did your child enjoy learning at home? Did you enjoy being the teacher?" If your experience was painful or stressful, a return to brick-and-mortar schooling may be a better idea.

Second, Mitchell said, think about the academic progress your child made at home. What subjects are coming up? If you're not a math whiz—and Mitchell has readily admitted she was not—can you either learn the math your child is going to need to know or find some way for them to be taught that content? "You are the one who's operating on the honor system. If you cheat, you're only cheating your child," she said. "Sooner or later they need to know this content." She found volunteers in the community who could help with the more advanced math lessons, and there are also plenty of online tutorials like the Khan Academy that can help.

Some parents found that their child made two or more years of progress during the time they were at home. Perhaps the classroom contained too many distractions for them to focus. Perhaps the teacher didn't have high expectations for them. But at home, they were able to master content they hadn't learned in school.

You do need to think about what you'll be giving up if you homeschool. What about social interaction? For some students, the social aspects of school are even more important than academics. If you're pulling them out, how are you going to make sure they still have friends and a peer group?

How will you provide enrichment activities like sports and music? "Homeschool families have their own community," Mitchell said. Join a homeschooling parent group, and you will learn about computer classes, theater classes, and even sports leagues that your child can join.

It's certainly not for everyone. But learning at the kitchen table may become a permanent school solution for your family.

14. SOME PARENTS ARE PUTTING TOGETHER A "LEARNING POD." ARE THESE A GOOD IDEA?

As the "temporary school closures" of the spring of 2020 stretched into the next school year, some families made the decision that they could no longer take on the entire responsibility of learning at home. Often, they joined with other families to create a "learning pod"—a small number of children working with a teacher or tutor for some or all of the day.

Parents turned to a learning pod for many reasons. They wanted their kids to be able to interact with other students their same age. They weren't sure that a full day of online learning was best for their child. And sometimes, they just had their own work to do.

Learning pods aren't cheap. Parents should expect to pay between $30 and $100 per hour per child, according to experts. That expense raises concerns that learning pods may accelerate the learning disparities among students when they return to in-person schooling.

This manuscript was completed about two weeks after the first learning pods started operating, so it seems early to draw any conclusions. But it is clear that parents will continue to look for ways to provide support for their child.

15. MY CHILD ATTENDS SCHOOL REMOTELY. I DON'T WANT THEM TO FALL TOO FAR BEHIND. HOW DO PARENTS KNOW WHAT SKILLS ARE MOST IMPORTANT IN EACH GRADE LEVEL?

Every year, teachers look at the list of content standards they are expected to cover in a year and think, "There's no way I can get all that done." Throughout the year, lesson planning feels like a constant game of Whack-a-Mole as teachers try to meet as many standards as possible.

Imagine, then, the feelings of parents who found themselves with no training in pedagogy, only a vague memory of what they had learned in each grade, and such lousy connectivity with the school that teachers couldn't provide much help on what was most important even if they wanted to.

So for help in planning their lessons, parents turned, naturally, to Pinterest. As a stopgap measure, there were probably worse places to go. But if at-home learning is going to become a regular thing, parents need help in sorting out what their kids really need to know so they can focus on that.

One of the most useful resources for parents and families was developed by the nonprofit organization Seek Common Ground (SCG) and the experts at Student Achievement Partners. They created Family Guides to help parents, grandparents, caregivers, friends—anyone helping a child to learn in the 2020–2021 school year—understand more about what children should know and be able to do by the end of each grade in literacy and math. That information, by grade level from kindergarten through Grade 8, is reprinted here with permission.

You may look these over and say, "But where's writing a haiku?" (Or memorizing a poem. Or, who knows, figuring baseball batting averages.) And you'd be right that this listing leaves out many things that teachers teach and students need to learn.

But hey, if you're stuck at your kitchen table and you have to focus on a few things that you *know* your kid should learn, then this is a darn good list. And it sure beats Pinterest.

If you want even more information on this topic, go to https://seek-commonground.org/family-guides. Note that these are the topics students are expected to master by the end of the year, so don't panic if your child can't do them all in October.

Kindergarten Key Content—Literacy

Learning to read and write:

- Playing with language, rhyming, clapping out or counting syllables. Identifying beginning, middle, and end sounds in spoken words.
- Naming all upper- and lower-case letters. Matching those letters with their sounds. Printing them clearly.
- Matching letters and sounds to sound out and write simple words. Focus on the most common consonant and short vowel sounds. (This may include inventive spelling for writing.)
- Reading and rereading decodable words and sentences in simple texts so the reading is smooth.

Learning about the world through text:✶

- Asking and answering questions about stories and texts read aloud. (Children may need some prompting.) Retelling what happened and explaining key ideas.
- Figuring out the meaning of unknown words by using pictures, context, etc. (Children may need support with pronunciation.)
- Showing something new they have learned from text or about a topic. This can be in lots of ways: speaking and conversation, illustrations, letters, journals, stories, posters, or sentences on the page.
- Using a combination of drawing, dictating, and writing to answer a question or describe an event or topic from a text. Children may use simple sentences and some inventive spelling.

✶The texts used for this purpose are often read aloud since they are more complex than the child could read alone. But texts children can read for themselves (with support as needed) may also be used.

First-Grade Key Content—Literacy

Learning to read and write:

- Matching letters and sounds to sound out and write simple words. (This may include inventive spelling for writing.) Students should be able to accurately decode and write all words with short vowel sounds, final -e, and common long vowel spellings.
- Recognizing, spelling, and properly using those little grammatical words that hold the language together (for example, "a," "the," "to," "of," "from," "I," "is," "are").
- Reading and rereading decodable words and sentences so that the reading is smooth.
- Writing in complete sentences.

Learning about the world through text:

- Accurately asking and answering questions about stories and texts read aloud. Retelling what happened and explaining key ideas.
- Figuring out the meaning of unknown words by using pictures, context, glossaries, etc. (Children may need support with pronunciation.)

- Showing something new they have learned from a text or about a topic. This can be in any form: speaking and conversation, illustrations, letters, journals, stories, posters, or sentences on the page.
- Using a combination of drawing and writing to describe an event in a text. Children should include a title, an introductory sentence, examples, and a conclusion sentence.

Second-Grade Key Content—Literacy

Learning to read and write:

- Matching letters and sounds to sound out and write most words. (This may include inventive spelling for writing.) Students should be able to accurately decode and write most commonly spelled one- and two-syllable words.
- Recognizing, spelling, and properly using those little grammatical words that hold the language together (for example, "a," "the," "to," "of," "from," "I," "is," "are").
- Reading and rereading decodable texts and words/sentences independently so that the reading is smooth.
- Reading grade level texts smoothly and with expression, at a fluency rate of between 70 and 130 words per minute by the end of the year.
- Writing complete sentences, with mostly correct spelling, capitalization, and punctuation.

Learning about the world through text:

- Asking and answering questions about stories and texts that are read aloud to them or they read to themselves. Retelling what happened and explaining key ideas.
- Figuring out the meaning of unknown words by using pictures, context, glossaries, etc. (Children may need support with pronunciation.) Figuring out the meaning of words in context when a known prefix or suffix is used ("happy/unhappy"; "pain/painful/painless").
- Showing something new they have learned from a text or about a topic. This can be in any form: speaking and conversation, illustrations, letters, journals, stories, posters, or sentences on the page.
- Writing about what happened or information learned from the text. Children should include a title, an introduction, well-developed examples, and a concluding statement or section.

Third-Grade Key Content—Literacy

Learning to read and write:

- Matching letters and sounds to sound out and write out most words. Students should be able to decode accurately and write words with several syllables and know and use suffixes and prefixes.
- Writing complete sentences and simple paragraphs about what they are learning, with mostly correct spelling, capitalization, and punctuation.
- Reading grade level texts smoothly and with expression, at a fluency rate of around 80–140 words per minute.

Learning about the world through text:

- Asking and answering questions about stories and texts read independently. Retelling what happened, explaining key ideas, and describing connections between ideas. Showing text evidence that supports their thinking.
- Figuring out the meaning of unknown words in text by using context or tools like dictionaries and glossaries. Determining or clarifying the meaning of unknown words, words with multiple meanings, or figurative language in context.
- Using linking words and phrases to connect ideas (such as "also," "another," "more," "but").
- Showing something new they have learned from a text or about a topic. This can be in any form: speaking and conversation, illustrations, letters, journals, stories, posters, or sentences on the page.
- Writing about what happened or information learned from the text. Children should include a title, an introductory sentence or section, well-developed examples, and a conclusion sentence or section.

Fourth-Grade Key Content—Literacy

Reading and writing skills:

- Writing to complete sentences and paragraphs about what they are learning, with mostly correct spelling, grammar, capitalization, and punctuation.

- Reading fourth grade-level texts smoothly and with expression, at a fluency rate of around 90–140 words per minute.

Learning about the world through text:

- Asking and answering questions about stories and texts read independently. Using specific evidence to describe, to explain how ideas are connected, and to support inferences about the text.
- Figuring out the meaning of unknown words in text by using context or tools like dictionaries and glossaries. Determining or clarifying the meaning of unknown words, words with multiple meanings, synonyms, antonyms, or figurative language in context.
- Linking opinions and reasons or ideas within categories using words and phrases to connect ideas (for example, "for instance," "in order to," "in addition," "for example," "also").
- Showing something new they have learned from a text or about a topic. This can be in any form: speaking and conversation, illustrations, letters, journals, stories, posters, or essays.
- Writing about what happened or information learned from the text. Children should include a title, an introductory sentence or section, well-developed examples, and a conclusion sentence or section. Spelling, capitalization, and punctuation should be mostly accurate.

Fifth-Grade Key Content—Literacy

Reading and writing skills:

- Writing to complete sentences and well-developed paragraphs about what they are learning, with mostly correct spelling, grammar, capitalization, and punctuation.
- Reading grade level texts smoothly and with expression, at a fluency rate of around 100–150 words per minute.

Learning about the world through text:

- Asking and answering questions about stories and texts read independently. Using specific evidence to support in-depth description, to explain how ideas are connected, and to support inferences about the text.

- Figuring out the meaning of unknown words in text by using context, word relationships, or tools such as dictionaries and glossaries. Determining or clarifying the meaning of unknown words such as synonyms, antonyms, idioms, and words with multiple meanings, based on how they are used in context.
- Linking opinions and reasons or ideas within categories using words and phrases (for example, "consequently," "specifically," "in contrast," "especially").
- Showing something new they have learned from a text or about a topic. This can be in any form: speaking and conversation, illustrations, letters, journals, stories, posters, or essays.
- Writing in response to text. Children should include an introduction with a simple thesis statement, examples that are logically ordered and grouped, a conclusion, and mostly accurate spelling, capitalization, and punctuation.

Sixth-Grade Key Content—Literacy

Reading, writing, speaking, and listening:

- Reading grade level texts smoothly and with expression, at a fluency rate of around 110–160 words per minute by the end of the year.
- Asking and answering questions about stories and texts read independently. Summarizing what happened in what was read and citing specific evidence to show how they know. Questioning the author's or speaker's assumptions. Determining the accuracy of statements they have heard or read.
- Analyzing the author's specific word choice to understand how it impacts the meaning or tone of the text. Determining or clarifying the meaning of unknown words, synonyms, antonyms, and figures of speech (for example, cause and effect, part and whole, item and category), and words with similar, but not identical, meanings (stingy, scrimping, economical, thrifty) based on how they are used in context, through word relationships, or by using tools like dictionaries or glossaries.
- Making and justifying a claim or line of argument in writing or discussion. Supporting claims with precise and relevant evidence from credible sources.

- Showing something new they have learned from a text or about a topic. This can be in any form: speaking and conversation, letters, journals, stories, diagrams, reports, or essays, with sufficient additional detail that fits the form they have chosen.
- Writing in response to text, including an introduction and thesis statement; examples that are linked, logically ordered and grouped; a conclusion; and mostly accurate spelling, capitalization, and punctuation.

Seventh-Grade Key Content—Literacy

Reading, writing, speaking, and listening:

- Reading grade level texts smoothly and with expression, at a fluency rate of around 170 words per minute by the end of the year.
- Asking and answering questions about stories and texts read independently. Summarizing what happened in what was read, analyzing how events or ideas are related, and citing specific evidence to show how they know. Questioning the author's or speaker's assumptions. Determining the accuracy of statements they have heard or read.
- Citing several sources of specific evidence from the text when analyzing a book, essay, article, or play in discussion or in writing.
- Evaluating the key points in something they read or hear. Asking questions. Stating their own well-supported ideas in writing or speaking.
- Determining or clarifying the meaning of unknown words, synonyms and antonyms, figures of speech (literary, biblical, mythological allusions), and words with similar, but not identical meaning (refined, respectful, polite, diplomatic, condescending) based on how they are used in context, through word relationships, or by using tools like dictionaries or glossaries.
- Making and justifying a claim or line of argument in writing or discussion. Supporting claims with precise and relevant evidence from credible sources.
- Showing something new they have learned from a text or about a topic. This can be in any form: speaking and conversation, letters, journals, stories, diagrams, reports, or essays, with sufficient additional detail that fits the form they have chosen.

- Writing in response to text. Seventh graders should include an introduction and thesis statement; examples that are linked, logically ordered, and grouped; a conclusion; and mostly accurate spelling, capitalization, and punctuation.

Eighth-Grade Key Content—Literacy

Reading, writing, speaking, and listening:

- Reading grade level texts smoothly and with expression, at a fluency rate of around 175 words per minute by the end of the year.
- Asking and answering questions about stories and texts read independently. Summarizing what happened in what was read; analyzing how a text makes connections or distinctions between ideas, characters, or events; and citing specific evidence to show how they know. Questioning the author's or speaker's assumptions. Determining the accuracy of statements they have heard or read.
- Citing the evidence that most strongly supports an analysis of what is explicitly stated and/or implied from a book, article, poem, or play.
- Analyzing where materials on the same topic disagree on matters of fact, interpretation, or point of view.
- Determining or clarifying the meaning of unknown words, synonyms and antonyms, figures of speech (irony, puns), and words with similar but not identical meaning (bullheaded, willful, firm, persistent, resolute) based on how they are used in context.
- Making and justifying a claim or argument in writing or discussion. Supporting claims with precise and relevant evidence from credible sources. Demonstrating a thorough understanding of the topic or text.
- Showing something new they have learned from a text or about a topic. This can be in any form: speaking and conversation, letters, journals, stories, diagrams, reports, or essays, with sufficient additional detail that fits the form they have chosen.
- Writing in response to text. Eighth graders should include an introduction and thesis statement; examples that are linked, logically ordered, and grouped; a conclusion; and mostly accurate spelling, capitalization, and punctuation.

Kindergarten Key Content—Math

- Counting to 10. By the end of the year, children should be able to count to 100.
- Counting objects to tell how many there are.
- Comparing two groups of objects to tell which group, if either, has more. (Group size of up to 20.)
- Understanding which of two written numbers between 1 and 10 is greater (6 is greater than 2).
- Acting out addition and subtraction word problems. Drawing pictures to represent and solve the problems.
- Adding with a sum of 10 or less. Subtracting from a number 10 or less.
- Adding and subtracting very small numbers quickly and accurately $(3 + 1)$.

First-Grade Key Content—Math

- Solving addition and subtraction word problems starting within 10 and progressing to within 20. (For example, "Five apples were on the table. I ate some apples. Then there were three apples. How many apples did I eat?")
- Adding with a sum of 20 or less, and subtracting from a number 20 or less. A common strategy for these problems is based on the number 10. (For example, to add $9 + 4$, a student might first add 1 to 9, making 10, then add the remaining 3 to 10, making 13.) When subtracting, a student may use their addition knowledge. (For example, to solve $12 - 8$, if a student knows that $8 + 4 = 12$, then taking 8 away from 12 would mean 4 remain.)
- Mentally adding with a sum of 10 or less $(2 + 5)$. Mentally subtracting with a sum of 10 or less $(8 - 4)$. Students may also come to know some of these sums and differences from memory.
- Understanding what the digits mean in two-digit numbers (the number 42 refers to 4 tens and 2 ones).
- Understanding and practicing adding two, two-digit numbers by adding tens and tens and ones and ones $(41 + 27 = 60 + 8 = 68)$.
- Measuring lengths of objects by using a shorter object as a unit of length. (For example, "How many pencils long is this table leg?")

Second-Grade Key Content—Math

- Solving challenging addition and subtraction word problems with one or two steps. (For example, a "one-step" problem would be: "Lucy has 23 fewer apples than Julie. Julie has 47 apples. How many apples does Lucy have?")
- Mentally adding the sum of any two single-digit numbers (remembering that 7 + 9 = 16). Subtracting mentally with ease from a number 20 or less.
- Understanding what the digits mean in three-digit numbers (the number 342 refers to 3 hundreds, 4 tens, and 2 ones).
- Using understanding of place value to add and subtract three-digit numbers (811 − 367). Adding and subtracting two-digit numbers with ease (77 − 28).
- Measuring and estimating length in standard units.
- Solving addition and subtraction word problems involving length. (For example, "The pen is 2 cm longer than the pencil. If the pencil is 7 cm long, how long is the pen?")

Third-Grade Key Content—Math

- Remembering the product of any two single-digit numbers (remembering that 7 × 9 = 63). Dividing mentally with ease for problems within the times tables (56 ÷ 8 = 7).
- Solving two-step word problems using addition, subtraction, multiplication, and division. (For example, "You already have 12 pens. There are 5 new packs of pens with 6 pens in each pack. How many pens do you have now?")
- Beginning to multiply numbers with more than one digit (multiplying 9 × 80).
- Understanding the meaning of division. Relating division to multiplication. (For example, "I know that 63 ÷ 9 = 7 because I remember 7 × 9 = 63.")
- Understanding fractions as parts of wholes. For example, ¾ inch is the length of 3 of the parts when 1 inch is broken into 4 equal parts.
- Understanding fractions as numbers. This includes representing fractions and whole numbers on a number line diagram; equating whole numbers and fractions (% = 1 and 3 = ¾); and comparing fractions in simple cases where the numerators are equal or the

denominators are equal (2⁄8 is less than 6⁄8 because 2 parts of a given size are less than 6 parts of the same size).

Fourth-Grade Key Content—Math

- Using the four operations, solve multistep word problems that use whole numbers and have whole number answers, including problems where students make sense of remainders. (For example, "Four classes are going on a field trip. The classes each have 28 students. Buses hold 48 passengers. If all of the students, 4 teachers and 4 chaperones are going on the field trip, how many buses will they need?")
- Adding and subtracting multi-digit numbers with ease (23,647 – 5,265).
- Multiplying and dividing multi-digit numbers in problems with a limited number of digits (1,638 × 7 or 24 × 17; 6,966 ÷ 6).
- Understanding and applying equivalent fractions (recognizing that 1⁄4 is less than 3⁄8 because 1⁄4 equals 2⁄8, and 2⁄8 are less than 3⁄8).
- Adding, subtracting, and multiplying fractions in simple problems (2 3⁄4 – 1 1⁄4 or 3 × 5⁄8), and solving related word problems that include fractions in context. (For example, you are going to make cookies for a party. You need 2⁄3 cup sugar for one batch and decide to make 8 batches, so all your neighbors can have a cookie. How many cups of sugar do you need?)
- Understanding and explaining simple decimals in terms of fractions (rewriting 0.62 as 62⁄100).

Fifth-Grade Key Content—Math

- Multiplying multi-digit numbers with ease (1,638 × 753). Dividing multi-digit numbers in cases with a limited number of digits (6,951 ÷ 63 = 110 1⁄3).
- Adding and subtracting fractions with unlike denominators (2 1⁄4 – 1 1⁄3), and solving word problems that include fractions with unlike denominators.
- Multiplying fractions and mixed numbers, and dividing fractions in special cases. Solving word problems using these operations. (For example, finding the area of a city block that is 1⁄3 mile long by 1⁄5

mile wide; finding the size of a share if 9 people share a 50-pound sack of rice equally, or if 3 people share ½ pound of chocolate equally.)
- Calculating with decimals to the hundredths place (two places after the decimal).
- Understanding the concept of volume, and solving word problems that involve volume.
- Graphing points in the coordinate plane (two dimensions) to solve problems.

Sixth-Grade Key Content—Math

- Understanding ratios and rates, and solving problems involving proportional relationships. (For example, "If it took 7 hours to mow 4 lawns, then at that rate, how many lawns could be mowed in 35 hours? At what rate were lawns being mowed?")
- Dividing fractions and solving word problems related to dividing fractions. (For example, "You are making granola. One batch of granola requires ⅔ cup of nuts. How many batches can be made with 4 cups of nuts?")
- Using positive and negative numbers together to describe quantities. Understanding the ordering and absolute values of positive and negative numbers. Representing points in the coordinate plane that have positive and negative coordinates.
- Reading, writing, and manipulating algebra expressions by applying knowledge of how numbers work (for example, when adding numbers, the order doesn't matter, so $x + y = y + x$). Emphasizing equivalent expressions and using properties of addition and multiplication to rewrite $24x + 18y$ as $6(4x + 3y)$, or $y + y + y$ as $3y$.
- Understanding and using the process of solving simple equations (those with one unknown quantity or variable; $7x = 22$).
- Writing equations to solve word problems and describe relationships between quantities. (For example, the distance [D] traveled by a train over a period of time [T] might be expressed by an equation $D = 85T$, where D equals the distance in miles and T equals the time in hours. This equation could be used to find the time required for the train to travel 100 miles or to find the distance the train would travel in 1.5 hours.)

Seventh-Grade Key Content—Math

- Analyzing proportional relationships (for example, by graphing in the coordinate plane), and distinguishing proportional relationships from other kinds of mathematical relationships (for example, buying 10 times as many items will cost you 10 times as much, but taking 10 times as many aspirin will not lower your fever 10 times as much).
- Solving percent problems including but not limited to tax, tips, and markups and markdowns.
- Adding, subtracting, multiplying, and dividing positive and negative numbers, and solving related word problems.
- Solving word problems that have a combination of whole numbers, fractions, and decimals. (For example, an employee making $25 per hour receives a 10% raise. The employee will make an additional $\frac{1}{10}$ of $25 per hour, or $2.50, for a new salary of $27.50.)
- Solving equations such as $\frac{1}{2}(x - 3) = \frac{3}{4}$ quickly and accurately, and writing equations of this kind to solve word problems. (For example, "I knocked over a carton of milk, and 3 cups were spilled before I set the carton upright again. When I poured out the remaining milk equally into two measuring cups, there was $\frac{3}{4}$ of a cup of milk in each one. How much milk was there originally?")

Eighth-Grade Key Content—Math

- Applying properties of integer exponents to generate equivalent expressions, using square roots to represent solutions to equations.
- Solving linear equations in one variable ($-x + 5(x + \frac{1}{3}) = 2x - 8$). (For example: "You rent a bike for $10 for the first hour, and each additional hour is $5.50. What is the cost of renting the bike for 6 hours?")
- Analyzing and solving systems of linear equations ($x + 6y = -1$ and $2x - 2y = 12$), emphasizing the real-world reasons these equations were created.
- Understanding functions (rules that assign to each input exactly one output); analyzing functions represented in different ways (for example, table, graph, verbal description, equation); interpreting equations for linear and nonlinear functions by graphing; and using functions to solve real-world problems. (For example, "Analyze and graph a company's profit over a set number of months. If in

one month a company profited $1,200, what is the slope or change when after five months the company profits $5,800?")

- Applying the Pythagorean Theorem ($a^2 + b^2 = c^2$) to solve real-world problems.

These standards are not everything a student should know, but students who have mastered them will at least know the basic content that their college classmates are likely to have been taught. You may also want to use a reading list to be sure your child has read books that college classmates will have studied. In a National Public Radio interview, Supreme Court Justice Sonia Sotomayor talked about what it was like to get to Princeton to realize that she simply had never read many of the things her classmates had read:

> One day talking to my first-year roommate . . . I was telling her about how out of place I felt at Princeton, how I didn't connect with many of the experiences that some of my classmates were describing, and she said to me, "You're like Alice in Wonderland."
> And I said, "Who is Alice?"
> And she said, "You don't know about Alice?"
> And I said, "No, I don't."
> And she said, "It's one of the greatest book classics in English literature. You should read it."[11]

Many teachers post their entire syllabus (the list of what they plan to teach) online. You can compare what your teen's school expects them to read with this list of recommended reading. It's not worth revisiting the entire Common Core fight, but the reading list developed to support those standards is comprehensive, ranging from Homer to Maya Angelou and from Jhumpa Lahiri to Oscar Wilde, and may be one you want to explore. You'll find it in the endnote.[12]

Once school went virtual, it exposed a divide that had existed for many years. The United States could no longer ignore the fact that 5 million homes with school-age children had no access to the internet.[13] The children affected were disproportionately poor, rural, and living in a household with a single parent.

Daniel Domenech, executive director of AASA, the School Superintendents Association, acknowledged the challenge that schools faced when learning suddenly left the school building for students' homes. "The reality is that probably the majority of school districts, and there are more than 13,000 of them, don't have the ability to provide continuous virtual online instruction." And while he believes that the push toward virtual learning has been accelerated, he noted that "right now it is definitely inequitable for students without internet access or a computer at home, and inequitable for the special-education population."

Long before the spring of 2020, 70% of teachers reported that they assigned homework that required broadband connectivity. Yet statistics from the Pew Research Center found that 1 in 4 lower-income teens had no access to a computer at home.[14]

When schools were open, students cobbled together solutions, doing homework on their smartphones, staying after school to work in the library, or learning the location of every nearby coffee shop and fast-food restaurant with free internet access.

But the school closure brought all those struggles to light. Some districts took action to expand digital access for their students, as described in Question 11. They distributed school computers to children who did not have them at home. (The Bergen County, New Jersey, schools, adopted this approach.) The Austin, Texas, schools were among the districts nationwide that parked school buses equipped with Wi-Fi hotspots in neighborhoods without broadband access. Employers and foundations raced to purchase computers and tablets. These efforts were bolstered by federal funding designed to address the digital divide.

But even with all that work, too many children were left behind. So the top priority for everyone must be to ensure that when the next closure comes, every student will be able to learn online.

That's not something an individual parent can do. But it is something that can happen when parents mobilize and take action. This book outlines ways parents can lead a campaign for change in Chapter 9, "What Parents Should Ask About Becoming Advocates for Change."

WHERE TO GET LEARNING HELP ONLINE

When you get stuck looking for a way to help your child, here are some online resources to check out. All are free.

ABCYA (https:// https://www.abcya.com/)
Games and activities designed to teach specific content in English language arts and math for grades K–5. All activities are linked to Common Core standards, but if your state does not use these standards, you will still be able

to find, for example, an activity to help a child determine the main idea in a reading passage. Science activities are also included.

Funbrain (https://funbrain.com)
Interactive games and videos in reading and math for pre-K through Grade 8. It's easy to search for activities that address specific topics or grade levels. The site also includes some fun games that reinforce learning concepts.

Illuminations (https:// https://illuminations.nctm.org/)
Developed by the National Council of Teachers of Mathematics, the site includes both lesson plans and activities tied to important math content. Activities are available for pre-K through Grade 12.

Khan Academy (https://khanacademy.org)
A wealth of lessons and activities designed to teach math K–12, as well as some more advanced classes in a variety of subjects . "Get ready" courses help students feel confident they are prepared for their next level math class. (The "Get ready for Algebra" class includes "Get ready for equations.") Other online activities help students enrolled in Advanced Placement classes. The activities on the site are all available for free.

Math for Love (www.mathforlove.com)
Math games and lessons, primarily for elementary grades.

Math Playground (https://www.mathplayground.com)
The site offers online math games, logic puzzles, and problem-solving activities for students in grades 1–6. Started by a teacher, the site helps parents find games to teach specific math skills. The games are linked to Common Core state standards, but parents can find the standard that applies to the content their child needs to learn.

Reading Rockets (https://readingrockets.org/audience/parents)
Developed by PBS, Reading Rockets includes a wealth of reading-related activities for kids and parents. From choosing a book to supporting children with autism while learning at home, the site includes helpful content for parents and fun things for kids to do.

3

QUESTIONS PARENTS SHOULD ASK ABOUT KINDERGARTEN

All children start their school careers with sparkling imaginations, fertile minds, and a willingness to take risks with what they think.

—Sir Ken Robinson

"It's bigger than I remembered," Sara said as we walked up to the front door of her elementary school on the first day of kindergarten. Her steps got slower and her eyes grew bigger. Although we had visited the school earlier, today seemed both more real and more intimidating.

Truth to tell, Sara was not the only one feeling intimidated. The first day of school is a parental milestone almost as enormous as it is for a child. That morning, I had reread Howard Nemerov's wonderful poem "September, the First Day of School." I, too, had a hard time letting go.

We found Sara's classroom—no easy task—and her kindergarten teacher instantly got her involved with an activity. Then the formidable Maryanne Nash, who had helped hundreds of parents and children deal with their first-day jitters, fixed a firm glance in my hovering direction. "We'll be fine," she said and looked pointedly at the door. As I took her cue and left, I knew they would be.

But while Sara was learning lessons, so was I. I learned that my child could find her own way in a classroom filled with kids she didn't know. I learned an even greater respect for the job of kindergarten teachers, who guide children as they begin to see themselves as learners. And I learned how I could work with the school in a way that helped both my child and the other students in her school.

Every year, more than 3.7 million children enter a kindergarten classroom for the first time. Another 1.4 million attend a public school pre-K program.[1] And on the first day of school, for virtually every one of them, there's a nervous parent worrying about whether the child is prepared for what comes next.

Over the years, starting with the Perry Preschool Project research in the early 1960s, researchers have examined what it takes to help a young child become successful in school. One theme has carried through all that research: the critical role of the parent.

Chapter 1 talks about both the research that confirms your critical role and the things you can do to build the strongest partnership between home and school. For preschoolers and kindergarteners, here are some additional questions to ask as you make important decisions about when and where your child will start kindergarten.

16. HOW DO I KNOW IF MY CHILD IS READY FOR KINDERGARTEN?

There is no question that today's kindergarten classroom has changed. In many states, children are expected to be reading at least some common words by the end of the year. In math, they will learn to add and subtract numbers up to 10 and to count to 100.

So a child who has never been read to, or who has never counted the steps to the mailbox, will have some serious catching up to do. But kindergarten teachers are prepared for that and know how to help children experience success.

A bigger key to success in kindergarten is whether children can focus on a project long enough to complete it, listen to a story as it is read by the teacher, or do detailed work like cutting and pasting. They need to be quiet when the teacher is talking. They have to adapt to a class routine and share attention with others. And they need to take pride in their ability to do things for themselves, whether that means tying their shoes, putting things away, or controlling their anger when they don't get their own way.

Lindsay Arnold is a kindergarten teacher who has taught children who were ready for kindergarten from the start, and she's taught some who weren't. It isn't so much that the former group has all the academic skills, she said. It's their ability to fit into a classroom filled with other children. "I've had a child walk through the door who didn't know one letter or number, but they fit right in," she said. "They waved goodbye to their parent, sat down, and listened to the rules. I can *teach* children their letters."

On the other hand, there are some children who have never had to share or take turns. "I taught one little boy who just melted down every time he didn't get his way, even if it was only that he wasn't called on first every time," Arnold said.

Parents can help by getting their child ready to learn in a room filled with other children. "We have lots of procedures in kindergarten—lining up before we leave the room, raising our hands before we talk, taking turns with toys and materials," she said. Children who have attended preschool are used to those routines, but parents can ease the way for the children just starting school. "Talk with your children about what to expect," she said. "Say, 'If you're going somewhere, you'll probably have to wait in a line.'" Arnold, who may have been destined to be a kindergarten teacher from the beginning, said she was prepared for this part of school. "I'm pretty sure I put my stuffed animals in a line and read to them."

Here are other skills your child will need in kindergarten and through-out their school career:

- Sharing. At home, your child may be the only one who wants to use the crayons or the building blocks. At school, several children may want to do those things.
- Taking turns. Similar to sharing, but this skill involves a toy or object that can be used by only one person at a time. Children need to understand that they can take a turn reading *The Very Hungry Caterpillar* or swinging on the swing, but they can't all do those things at the same time.
- Accepting no. Apparently, there are some parents who manage to parent a child for five years without ever telling them no. So here's a news flash: It will happen in kindergarten. Children need to know how they can respond to the disappointment of being unable to do what they want.
- Listening and following directions. This is a skill that children will use from kindergarten right through high school. At home, you might try giving your child one- or two-step directions to see if they can follow them. ("Please put this pile of folded laundry on your bed." "Please take this cup to the kitchen and bring back an apple for each of us.")
- Following rules and procedures. Whether your child is playing soccer or sitting in a classroom, they are going to have to follow rules. You probably already have some family rules, and you might

involve your child in reviewing them and perhaps making some changes.

Readiness for school does not mean that your child will do everything right. Instead, it means that your child will take pleasure in learning how to do things on their own. If you always do things for your child, and always tell them what to do, they will not be able to make their own decisions and learn how to be independent.

If you want to make sure your child is "ready" for kindergarten, focus on the skills the teacher needs you to teach. As Lindsay Arnold said, they can teach your child the ABCs. They can't teach them (or at least not very efficiently) to accept that they won't get their way all the time.

17. MY CHILD IS OFF TO KINDERGARTEN IN THE FALL. HOW CAN I HELP MY CHILD LEARN TO DO THINGS LIKE TYING THEIR SHOES BEFORE KINDERGARTEN?

Presumably, you are not planning to attend kindergarten again. So that means that your child is going to have to do some things independently. Kindergarteners are expected to take responsibility for their own belongings. They put their lunch box in the right place. They hang up their coat. During the day, they use the restroom and wash their hands by themselves. They take out and put away supplies they need.

In the cafeteria, children have to put the straw in their juice box or open the milk carton. They have to get the foil top off the applesauce. "The whole first month in the cafeteria, we're helping children learn to open things," Arnold said. "They are always surprised that ketchup packages have a little line that shows you where to tear to get the ketchup out." So teach your child how to do that before the first day of school.

One of the most important ways to help your child be ready for kindergarten is by teaching them how to do things for themselves. Whenever possible, avoid doing things for your child that they can do on their own. Let your toddler feed themselves (and accept that mealtime will be messy and s-l-o-w, at least at first). Let young children choose what they want to wear—and relax if they choose to wear the polka-dot shirt with the checked pants. Encourage them to use the crayons they want to use in their coloring book, and do not be surprised if you see a purple horse or a red elephant.

Follow the rule that teachers use when they are teaching a new skill:
First I do.
Then we do.
Then you do.

Whether it's shoe tying or making a sandwich, start by showing your child what to do. Then practice the same skill together, working side by side. Finally, let your child do it alone, first while you watch and then independently.

And let me just say one word here about shoes—the bane of every kindergarten teacher. Shoelaces do not stay tied. "They drag on the floor. They drag across the restroom floor. They go into kids' mouths," Arnold said. "Then they need my help retying them. If I have 25 students, that's 50 feet. And at 30 seconds per shoe tie, that's 25 minutes a day I'm not teaching them letters or numbers or how to get along with others," she said.

"That doesn't mean children have to be able to tie their shoes before they start kindergarten," she said. "Just put them in different shoes." And really, just reread that part about shoelaces that have dragged on the kindergarten restroom floor ending up in the child's mouth. You'll probably keep your kid in Velcro shoes until they're 20.

Kids do eventually learn how to tie shoes. Sara started kindergarten wearing shoes with Velcro closings because she couldn't tie shoelaces. At the end of the year, her teacher told me, "She came into kindergarten missing only one skill, and she's about to leave kindergarten still missing that same skill. I am certainly not going to keep her from going to first grade because she can't tie her shoes, but she eventually will have to learn."

And then one day, in a shoe store, Sara saw a pair of shoes she really loved. "I'm not buying those," I said. "They're tie shoes and you don't know how to tie them."

"Show me," she said. So we sat down on the floor of the shoe store, and in about five minutes, she mastered it.

Young children can do more than you think. One helpful list of life skills to teach children at any age was written by Lindsay Hutton and published on the Family Education Network website. Check out the whole list, but here are the things she said that a 4- or 5-year-old should be able to do:

• perform simple cleaning chores like dusting in easy-to-reach places and clearing the table after meals;
• feed pets;

- identify money denominations and understand the very basic concept of how money is used;
- brush her teeth, comb her hair, and wash their face without help;
- help with basic laundry chores, such as putting her clothes away and
  bringing her dirty clothes to the laundry; and
- choose their own clothes to wear[2]

All of these seem like small things for your child to do for themselves. But they will provide a foundation that will let them make small choices and then live with the consequences. They will let them take charge of some parts of their life from an early age. And they will help them learn how to take on bigger choices as they grow older.

18. SHOULD I "REDSHIRT" MY CHILD (KEEP THEM OUT OF KINDERGARTEN FOR ANOTHER YEAR)?

My daughter went to high school with a football player who was recruited by the nationally ranked Virginia Tech football team. But he didn't play for the Hokies during his first year in Blacksburg. He was "redshirted"—held off the team for a year so he could get bigger and stronger. For Sara's friend, redshirting worked—he played four years for Virginia Tech, graduated with a double major, and went on to a successful NFL career.

But the practice of "redshirting" also applies to kindergartners. During the past decades, it has become more common for parents to hold their kids out of school for an extra year. Nationally, about 9% of parents hold their children out for an extra year, according to the National Center for Education Statistics.[3] Typically, kids who are redshirted are more likely to be boys, particularly boys who have birthdays in the last half of the year. The practice is also twice as common in schools serving affluent student bodies as in those serving low-income families.[4]

Parents who hold their kids out (or schools that make redshirting an easy option) do so because they think it gives these kids an advantage. They hope children will be more ready for school—academically, physically, and socially. The practice was highlighted in Malcolm Gladwell's best-selling book *Outliers*. The book is an examination of the factors that lead some people to become high achievers. Particularly as he looked at hockey players who rose to play on highly competitive junior hockey teams, Gladwell noted that nearly all of them had birthdays earlier in the year. So they were older than other students in their kindergarten class.

For the first few years of school, redshirting does appear to give children an academic boost. Older kindergarteners score on average 24 percentage points higher on standardized reading tests than their younger classmates. But over time, those gains start to erode. By eighth grade, the younger students have virtually caught up—older students score just 4 points higher. A study in the *Journal of Human Resources* suggests the trade-offs might not be worth it.[5]

"If it were true that older kids are able to learn at a faster rate, then the differences in test scores should get bigger as kids progress and the material gets more difficult. But we really see the opposite," said Darren Lubotsky, an economist at the University of Illinois and a coauthor of the study.

"It's clear the pattern is these academic differences get smaller as kids get older," Lubotsky noted. "It doesn't seem reasonable to us that there could be large long-term gains from starting kindergarten at an older age when there isn't much of an effect for kids in eighth grade."[6]

There's also some evidence that teens who were redshirted in kindergarten have more behavior problems than their classmates—and that they are more likely to end up in special education.[7] Taken together, these studies may indicate that the behaviors that parents and teachers sometimes think of as "immaturity" may in fact be undiagnosed learning problems.[8]

Fairfax County, Virginia, parents Renee and Justin Lang considered whether they should redshirt their daughter Evelyn because she was born in September, and she would be one of the youngest in her class. "We knew she was strong in the academic areas. There she was definitely ready for kindergarten," Renee said. But there were other areas where Evelyn still had room to grow and develop. "Most of the work she needed to do was in the area of social skills—being attentive in class, things of that nature," she said.

They talked with other parents and met with the school. They realized that "kindergarten teachers are experienced with this. They know how to provide individualized support." In addition, Renee said, "We knew that spending a year on the sidelines was not going to fix any of those things. And if she stayed in preschool for another year, she'd just be bored." They signed her up for kindergarten and are very happy they did.

What does this research mean for you if your child is about to enter kindergarten? Should you redshirt your child? As with so many other things in parenting, the right answer is: It depends. But here are questions to ask yourself before you make the decision to keep your child out of kindergarten for a year:

- Why exactly do you think your child should be held out a year? There are characteristics that can have an effect on kindergarten success—things like an inability to sit still or social immaturity. But don't hold a child back just because they have a birthday close to the cutoff or because they would be among the youngest in the class.
- What are the school's expectations? There's no question that kindergarten is more academic today than ever. But there are things parents can do to help children prepare. At the kindergarten roundup or when you register your child, ask about expectations for entering kindergartners.
- Does your state have any programs to help young children transition from preschool to kindergarten? If you live in California and you have a child who would be young for kindergarten, you might investigate the state's transitional kindergarten program. This two-year program is part of the state's public K–12 education system. It teaches a modified kindergarten curriculum spread across both years and is available for all children in California who have their fifth birthday between September 2 and December 2. California is the only state to have adopted this approach, but other states may offer other transitional programs to help your child.

  What does your child's preschool teacher think? She is able to give a much more objective evaluation of your child's kindergarten readiness when compared with other children the same age. Ask questions like these:
  o Did my child make friends in preschool?
  o Were they able to follow directions?
  o Do you think they are ready for the academic work in kindergarten?
- What kind of a kindergarten class will your child enter? Is it organized around learning centers? This structure is one way to help students at a variety of developmental levels be successful. If your child can't sit still, they are less likely to be successful in a kindergarten classroom that teaches all children in a formal, more structured way. Is the kindergarten class size likely to be larger than 25? A very shy child might find a large class more difficult to adjust to than they would a class of around 20 or fewer. Class size may be a more important consideration for a shy child than even for a child who is not shy but who lacks physical coordination.

- What else will your child do if they're not in school? Is there a good preschool program that will continue to help them develop academically? Will they still be able to play with their friends?
- What is the latest date by which you have to decide? A child who seems immature in April may be very different by September. If you are considering keeping your child out of kindergarten, make that decision as late as you possibly can.

19. HOW DO I CHOOSE THE RIGHT KINDERGARTEN FOR MY CHILD?

In many communities, finding the kindergarten your child will attend is simple: Your address determines school assignments. But in some places, parents have the option of choosing a school and a program that fits their child's needs. Other parents want to look at private schools or charter schools.

Trying to select from so many options can be confusing. Talking with other parents or with neighbors is a place to start—but your child may thrive in a classroom that is very different from one that works well for the child next door.

Here are some tips and questions for parents as you make a decision about the school and the program that would be best for your child:

- Schedule a visit. Many schools offer scheduled tours and visits for prospective students. Others will allow you to visit a classroom. However, you should not plan on just showing up. Schedule the visit in advance.
- Try to picture your child in the classroom. Are children spending most of their time playing and working with materials or other children? Do they move purposefully from one activity to another? When Janet Soller, a mother of five boys, went to story time at a school where she was considering enrolling her son James, she was struck by the sight of two little boys both standing on toy trucks and pretending to ice-skate. "I knew it wasn't the right school for Jimmy," she said. "Maybe if I'd had a kid who wasn't a risk taker. But James would have been right there on the trucks."
- Check out the resources that are available in the classroom. Good classrooms don't need every bell and whistle. But they do need to provide children with varied activities throughout the day. Look

for assorted building blocks and other construction materials, props for pretend play, picture books, paints and other art materials, and table toys such as matching games, pegboards, and puzzles. Children should not always be doing the same thing at the same time.

- Look at how teachers interact with children. Are teachers working with individual children, small groups, and the whole group at different times of the day?
- Ask how children learn numbers and the alphabet. Is it in the context of their everyday experiences? Does the natural world of plants and animals and meaningful activities like cooking, taking attendance, or serving a snack provide the basis for learning activities?
- Are there special programs available in the kindergarten or the school? Can children learn a second language? Participate in arts activities? Do hands-on science?
- Do children have an opportunity to play outside every day, weather permitting?
- Is the curriculum adapted for those who are ahead as well as those who need additional help? Do teachers recognize that children's different backgrounds and experiences mean that they do not learn the same things at the same time in the same way?

20. HOW CAN I
ENCOURAGE MY CHILD TO LOVE READING?

There's a reason that reading is the first of the three Rs. Reading is the foundation for virtually all other learning. And parents can play a critical role in helping children learn to love reading. A National Center for Education Statistics report summarized the results of many studies: "For decades, research has shown that children whose parents read to them become better readers and do better in school."[9]

Arnold has seen the same thing in her classroom. "Reading to your kids every day really does work," she said. Follow that up by talking about the books you're reading.

Keep it light and fun. Reading really can be magic, so treat it that way. Make reading at home an activity that everyone looks forward to. Sometimes drape a blanket over two chairs and create a reading tent (or a reading fort or a reading pirate ship, depending on your kids' imagination).

Make reading aloud a family routine. Reading aloud is one of the best ways to encourage a love of reading. It's never too early to get in the habit of reading—even babies love the sound of a parent's voice while they snuggle. It's also never too *late* to start reading. Many families find that even their middle or high school children love to hear parents read interesting stories aloud. Aim for 15 minutes a day, but understand there will be days when you may not hit that goal. You can get creative with when you do read aloud—some busy families combine reading with bath time. Others read aloud during breakfast.

Take your time. Reading aloud isn't a race to the finish. Stop and ask questions so your child will think about what you are reading. "What do you think Peter Rabbit will do next?" Get your child to talk about the characters in the book. Are they like people they know? And point out structure (beginning, middle, end). "You can also do that with TV shows, or with your day," Arnold said.

Choose books that you and your child enjoy. You never know which book is going to become a favorite that your child will want to hear over and over again. Try to choose things you enjoy. However, there will inevitably be a book that your child loves and you—well, you love much less. Once the attachment is formed, you'll just have to grin and go with it!

Pick a topic you and your child can learn about together. Read books, look online, do things together. You may become an expert on rocks . . . or the New York Mets . . . or the trees in your area. Both you and your child are likely to learn something new.

Read predictable books. These are books with a word or action that appears over and over. Children learn to predict what will happen next and that gives them a sense of mastering a particular book. These are often the first books that children can read by themselves.

Don't worry about what your child is reading. A child who is not interested in reading a book of fiction may be captivated by a book about rocks or dinosaurs or baseball. Nonfiction often is more appealing to boys than girls, and it is appealing to children who want to master facts. If your child plays a computer game or watches a favorite cartoon, you might find books based on those characters. They can be a good way to capture your child's attention. If you're worried because your child seems only to want to read comic books—hey, they're called "graphic novels" now, and even adults enjoy them. The point is that reading comes in many forms, so let your child find the one that appeals right now.

Include audible books. There are times when you can't read aloud—you're driving or cooking dinner, for example. That's when an audible book can be a great addition to your read-aloud program. A professional actor (or the author) will read the book, and everyone in the family can enjoy it. You can often download audible books for free from your local public library.

But skip e-readers for young readers. For many adult readers, an e-reader is a lifesaver—a way to store many books when you're going to be on a plane or headed out for a vacation. But most experts still suggest that the youngest readers should start reading with real books printed on real paper. There's not much research yet, but there is some evidence that children retain more of what they read from a book. A study in *Pediatrics* found that there were fewer parent–child interactions when parents read from e-books rather than from print.[10] However, kids with visual impairments may find the ability to adjust the size of the print on an e-book to be invaluable.

Encourage your child to read books with diverse characters. Every child needs to see themselves reflected in the pages of the books they read. If your child is a member of a racial or ethnic minority, make a special effort to find books that feature children who look like yours. Your school's librarian or your local public library's children's librarian can be an invaluable source of suggestions. White children, too, need to read books that are populated with characters who represent all nationalities. Children need to read about cultural traditions that they share, as well as some cultural traditions they know nothing about. They need to read stories about families like theirs and families that have different structures.

Leave books everywhere. Make it almost impossible for your child not to encounter a book. It goes without saying that you'll have some books in the bathroom. But why not set a book close to the microwave? And a beautiful picture book on a coffee table may attract your child's interest. Leave paperbacks or magazines anywhere they might catch your child's attention.

Get reacquainted with your local public library. "Libraries," said author Sidney Sheldon, "change lives for the better." Yes, libraries offer access to thousands of books. But they also often provide much more. Story hours can captivate toddlers and their parents. Author visits give readers a chance to interact with someone they have known only on the page. And summer reading programs can keep children challenged and engaged in learning even while school is out.

Make the day your child gets their first library card a special one. Author Rita Mae Brown said, "When I got my library card, that's when my life began." So treat the card as the milestone that it is.

Turn on closed captioning. It's an easy way to increase your child's exposure to print.

Books to read the summer before kindergarten

Sometimes, reading a book about kindergarten can make the first day of school seem a little more familiar. From a variety of teacher-recommended lists, I've assembled this rather extensive library. There are sure to be a couple of books your child enjoys.

- *Amanda Panda Quits Kindergarten* (Candice Ransom)
- *The Kissing Hand* (Audrey Penn)
- *Kindergarten ABC* (Jacqueline Rogers)
- *Kindergarten Kids* (Ellen B. Senisi)
- *Welcome to Kindergarten* (Anne Rockwell)
- *My Name Is Yoon* (Helen Recorvits)
- *Sumi's First Day of School Ever* (Soyung Pak)
- *Kindergarten Countdown* (Anna Jane Hays)
- *Countdown to Kindergarten* (Alison McGhee)
- *Froggy Goes to School* (Jonathan London)
- *On the Way to Kindergarten* (Virginia L. Kroll)
- *When You Go to Kindergarten* (James Howe)
- *Off to School, Baby Duck!* (Amy Hest)
- *I Am Not Going to School Today* (Robie H. Harris)
- *A Place Called Kindergarten* (Jessica Harper)
- *Meet the Barkers: Morgan and Moffat Go to School* (Tomie dePaola)
- *I'm Telling You, Dex, Kindergarten Rocks* (Katie Davis)
- *First Day Jitters* (Julie Danneberg)
- *Will I Have a Friend?* (Miriam Cohen)
- *I Am Too Absolutely Small for School* (Lauren Child)
- *Look Out Kindergarten, Here I Come* (Nancy Carlson)
- *The Berenstain Bears Go Back to School* (Stan Berenstain)
- *Tucker's Four-Carrot School Day* (Susan Winget)
- *Tom Goes to Kindergarten* (Margaret Wild)
- *My Kindergarten* (Rosemary Wells)
- *Amanda Pig, Schoolgirl* (Jean Van Leeuwen)
- *Mouse's First Day of School* (Lauren Thompson)
- *I Love School!* (Philemon Sturges)
- *Miss Bindergarten Gets Ready for Kindergarten* (Joseph Slate)
- *Annabelle Swift, Kindergartener* (Amy Schwartz)

Ask your local librarian for other suggestions.

21. MY CHILD OFTEN HAS A HARD TIME ADJUSTING TO NEW SITUATIONS. WHAT CAN I DO TO MAKE THE FIRST FEW WEEKS OF SCHOOL EASIER?

It's not unusual for children to worry about starting kindergarten. Even children who have been in preschool for a year or two can be concerned about what will happen when they go to the big kids' school. The key to helping your child adjust is to start early rather than waiting until the night before school opens. Talk about school: What do they think they'll like best? Share some of your memories of kindergarten. Read books about kindergarten. See the list in the textbox above.

Play "What if" games. What if I don't get to sit with my best friend? (Teachers often ask children to sit in certain seats. You can play with your friend later in the day.) What if I have a question about something and I don't understand what I'm supposed to do? (Raise your hand. Teachers know that kids have questions—it's how they learn.)

Choose a small, tangible object your child can keep in a backpack or a pocket. Or create a ritual that will remind your child of your love. The Langs read *The Kissing Hand* by Audrey Penn, a story about a little raccoon whose mother shares a family secret called the Kissing Hand. In the book, it was a reassurance of her love, and in real life, it was a way for Evelyn to remember that her mom and dad loved her even when she was at school and not with them.

An early start will also help your child adjust to a school schedule. If they're used to dawdling over breakfast and now they're going to have to catch a school bus, they need to practice a new routine so they're ready. And be sure they get into the habit of eating something nourishing in the morning. Little learners really do need food for their brains to kick into gear.

Setting a regular bedtime is critical. University of British Columbia sleep expert and nursing professor Wendy Hall recently led a review of a number of studies on children and sleep. "Research tells us that kids who don't get enough sleep on a consistent basis are more likely to have problems at school and develop more slowly than their peers who are getting enough sleep," she reported.[11]

As a kindergarten teacher, Lindsay Arnold tells parents to expect their children to be tired. "Those first six weeks, children will be exhausted," she said. So especially during the first month of school, "don't overbook them. Don't have them go to 18 activities." And if they come home from school and want a nap, let them rest for a while.

Meet the teacher. Most schools invite kindergarten students and their parents to visit the school before the first day. If at all possible, try to attend. Your child will feel more relaxed if they have been to the classroom and have met their teacher.

Children thrive on orderliness, and kindergarten classrooms cannot function without a firm but supportive structure. So create some routines—when you get up, when you eat lunch, when it's time to put away the toys for the day. It is, of course, possible to overdo this whole routine thing. (Checking out mom schedules on Pinterest will make you want to lie down and take a nap.) But getting into a regular pattern will make things easier when school starts.

If you have enjoyed a regular read-aloud time with your preschooler, keep that habit going. If you had fallen out of the habit, take time for a pre-bedtime book.

You will have some reading assignments as well. Be sure you read through any letters or instructions that were sent home from the school. And take that school calendar and transfer important dates—parent–teacher conferences, school holidays, the fall concert —to your family calendar.

In 1988, author Robert Fulghum published *All I Really Need to Know I Learned in Kindergarten*. The book remained on the best-seller list for more than two years. Clearly, Fulghum struck a nerve.

While it's hard to argue that kindergarten really teaches everything people really need to know, it is a place where children can build a strong foundation for school and for life. As a parent, you get to experience that with them. So take them to school on the first day. Read to them every night. Don't buy tie shoes unless you're really sure they can tie them by themselves. And enjoy the beginning of a journey that will take your child through college and into adulthood.

4

QUESTIONS PARENTS SHOULD ASK ABOUT ELEMENTARY SCHOOL

It is not what you do for your children, but what you have taught them to do for themselves, that will make them successful human beings.

—Ann Landers

For most families, the elementary school years are pretty calm. Kids mostly still like you. They usually like school. They are busy with friends and interests.

They're curious and willing to try new things. "They are full of hugs and laughter," said Andrew Ellingsen, a music teacher and instructional coach who has worked across the entire range of elementary grades. "If they feel loved and supported, they are willing to try anything."

But like a duck gliding across a pond, there's a lot of action where you can't see it. Physical changes are not as rapid as they will be during puberty, but they're happening. (After all, kids even leave elementary school with a completely different set of teeth than they started with!) Emotions may be hidden, but they do live fairly close to the surface, Ellingsen said. "It's not uncommon to see an elementary school child crying because she can't get her shoe tied." (And if you did not read Question 17 in Chapter 3, on why sending children to kindergarten in tie shoes is a very bad idea, it's worth heading there right now.)

Learning also progresses. The child who enters grade school able to count to 10 is likely to leave knowing how to multiply and divide fractions and solve equations. Developmentally, these are the years when children develop attitudes about schools and learning, including study habits, that remain relatively permanent throughout the remainder of their schooling.

Friends are important, although not as important as they will be in middle and high school. For most of elementary school, girls are friends with girls and boys are friends with boys.

Your child's elementary school years should be when they build a solid foundation for learning. They are the years when kids need to master the basics that will make all other learning possible. During these early years, children can also form habits (like taking responsibility for their belongings) and beliefs ("I can learn this") that will help them throughout the rest of their academic career.

Your influence is still enormous. Most children spend only 6 or 7 hours a day in school. The rest of the time they are still learning valuable lessons. When they play sports, they learn about teamwork and following rules. When they play with friends, they learn about getting along with others. The activities they choose for relaxation—reading, hobbies, and, yes, even online games—also affect what and how they learn. You as a parent have at least some influence over all those out-of-school activities. The value you place on education and the models you provide are constantly shaping your child's learning, even when they are not in school.

When parents and schools work together, it's easier for children to achieve success. But as parents, we're not born knowing how we can best help. We often have to struggle to find the right balance between letting our child find their own way and supporting the teacher and the school.

So don't be surprised if you find yourself asking questions about what you should do and what you should avoid. Here are 11 big questions parents should ask while their child is in elementary school.

22. WHAT'S THE MOST IMPORTANT THING I CAN DO TO HELP MY CHILD BE SUCCESSFUL IN ELEMENTARY SCHOOL?

There are a lot of possible answers to this question: being sure your child learns how to read, helping them learn how to get along with others, developing their self-esteem. And all of those are important tasks. But the single most important task for a parent is to start working yourself out of a job.

The list of things 5-year-olds do not know or cannot do is pretty lengthy. But according to psychologist Madeline Levine in *Teach Your Children Well*, the single most important job for parents is to start shortening that list. Elementary school students need "to move away from near-total dependence on the family for regulation . . . to increased *self*-regulation."[1]

Levine is talking about helping children learn to control their emotions, moving from "Tell your brother you're sorry you broke his truck" to "Hey, I'm sorry I broke your toy." But it's true in many other areas as well.

While kindergarten children are going to need a lot of help getting ready for school on time every day, older elementary students should be able to do that on their own. While young students need you to be close by when they do their homework, older students should be able to get most of their studying done by themselves.

It's only through their own experiences that kids learn to trust their intuition or their judgment. It's only by trying and failing that they learn how to try and not fail the next time.

But there seem to be more and more of the do-everything parents every day. Joan Reynolds, retired Fairfax County teacher, recalled seeing the breed increase dramatically. "That helicopter parent thing just got more and more out of control. Parents are just not willing to let kids learn any basic life lessons. They want them to get the A no matter what, and aren't willing to let their kids learn the skills they need to get the A." (See Question 5 in Chapter 1 for ways to tell if you are an overly involved helicopter parent.)

If you set only one goal for your child's elementary school years, strive to raise a child who will grow into an independent adult. That is, of course, unless you are planning to go to college right along with them. And apparently that's what the Varsity Blues parents would have had to do. But as it turns out, it's hard to make a college visit from jail.

23. HOW DO I CHOOSE THE RIGHT ELEMENTARY SCHOOL FOR MY CHILD?

Until fairly recently, about the only options available to parents choosing an elementary school were whether their children went to public school or a religious school. Today, families have many more choices. Within the public school system, parents can often choose an elementary school that best matches their child's interests—whether it's a focus on the arts, instruction in two languages, or a traditional approach that includes school uniforms. And of course, for families with some resources, "school choice" is always available by buying a home in a desired attendance area.

Many communities now include charter schools—publicly funded schools that operate independently. There are private schools, both religious and nonsectarian. And finally, families have the option of home-schooling their child.

How do you select the school that's right for your child?

Think about the needs of your child and your family. Consider what you want the school to do for your child. You know them best, and you'll know if they are likely to need a more structured learning environment or if they will do better in a school that provides a more unstructured approach.

But the needs of the child need to be balanced with the needs of the whole family. A perfect school that is a 90-minute drive from your house might be good for one child but bad for the family as a whole. Also consider your need for childcare before and after school.

Gather information about the schools on your list. All public schools make information available to the general public through a school report card. You'll find information about student achievement, school safety, teacher quality, and other topics of interest. (Use a search engine to find the report card for any public school you want to learn about.)

Look deeper to find out more about the curriculum the school offers—what courses can children take beyond the core academic subjects? Does the school offer arts programs? Physical education? Are there enrichment opportunities for all students?

If you are the parent of a special-needs child, be sure the school can meet their needs. Are specialized staff members available (e.g., speech therapist, psychologist, or aides)?

Of course you will want to look at test scores, but this should not be the primary focus of your research. Try to see what you can find about how children like yours are doing in the school. Sometimes, high average test scores mask the reality that not all students are doing equally well. If you are the parent of a Black or Brown student, see how those students compare to white peers.

Find out as much as you can about how the school works with parents. Does the school have a website that provides useful information? How do teachers communicate with parents? What is the school's policy about parent inquiries?

Visit the school if possible. How big are the classes? Do children seem to be engaged in productive learning? How do teachers treat children? How do children treat each other?

Consider school facilities. Learning can happen in many locations, but you want a school that has a good library, plenty of computers, and a playground where children can relax and let off steam.

If you are looking at a school that has an admission process, be sure you know the deadlines. If you are considering a private school, be sure you know not only the tuition but also the additional fees that may be required.

Good schools come in many shapes and sizes. From instruction in two languages to a Montessori curriculum to an arts or science focus, you may find a school that offers these components.

However, you should also think about what you are willing to do to make whichever school your child attends better. Research from North Carolina State University, Brigham Young University, and the University of California, Irvine, found that parental involvement is a more significant factor in a child's academic performance than the qualities of the school itself. "Our study shows that parents need to be aware of how important they are, and invest time in their children—checking homework, attending school events and letting kids know school is important," said Toby Parcel, a professor of sociology at NC State and coauthor of a paper on the work. "That's where the payoff is."[2]

24. MY CHILD IS STARTING FIRST GRADE AND DOESN'T KNOW HOW TO READ. SHOULD I WORRY?

Some parents panic if their child does not start first grade already knowing how to read. Even those who are calm at the start of first grade may get more anxious as the year progresses. Is there a "right" age for children to learn to read?

You'll be relieved to know that the answer is no. Children learn to walk at their own pace, to speak at their own pace, and, yes, to read at their own pace. So if you are taking steps to encourage your child to enjoy reading (including those in the last chapter), there's no need to panic if they are not reading by the time they start school.

The most helpful thing you can do for a pre-reader is to read aloud with your child every day. Then talk about what happened. If it's a story, see if they can retell it in their own words. If it's a factual text (about dogs or dinosaurs or a favorite cartoon character), see if they can tell you one thing they learned.

Even after children learn to read, encourage them to keep practicing. Reading is a skill, and just like other skills, it's refined with practice. Just as you read to your child, have them read to you.

When your child is first learning to read, offer to read every other page or every other chapter. As your child becomes a stronger reader, they won't want to be read *to*. They'll want to be read *with*. So ask them to read the part of one of their favorite characters in a book. Or say, "Why don't you read *me* a story?"

25. MY THIRD GRADER IS NOT READING
AT A THIRD-GRADE LEVEL. SHOULD I WORRY?

Parents of nonreading first graders don't need to worry. But there is a time when parents should get concerned—and it's by the time your child reaches the third grade. Research consistently shows that students who do not read on grade level by their third-grade year are facing serious academic headwinds for the rest of their life.

Children need to master two different aspects of reading in elementary school. First, they must learn to read—figuring out how to decode the words they see on a printed page. But they also need to *read to learn*. Every subject—from history to math—involves reading skills. So if your child is not reading, they will struggle learning the content in every subject and not just language arts.

In the primary grades, emphasis is on learning to read, and that's where most classroom instruction will be focused. But by third grade, teachers focus more on helping students understand what they read. So "reading" instruction is likely to focus on things like background knowledge and vocabulary.

But a child who is still struggling to sound out *c-a-t* isn't going to focus on the fact that tigers, lions, and leopards are all members of the same cat family. And that academic struggle will just get worse as the child moves through school.

One study of nearly 4,000 students found that children who are proficient in reading in third grade are 4 times more likely to graduate from high school than those who do not. In fact, 1 in 6 students who are not reading proficiently in third grade did not graduate from high school by age 19.[3]

For the students whose performance was the lowest—those who are said to have "below basic" reading skills—the graduation rates are even lower. Children with the lowest reading scores account for a third of students but for more than three-fifths (63%) of all children who do not graduate from high school.

Look at the results of the standardized tests the school gives your child. Pay special attention to their scores in reading. Then ask your child to read a passage from one of their textbooks aloud. If they struggle over even the simplest words, you should ask for a conference with the teacher.

26. MY CHILD NEVER PICKS
UP A BOOK. HOW CAN I HELP A READER
WHO AVOIDS READING AT ALMOST ALL COSTS?

There are two reasons most kids avoid reading. Some are *reluctant* readers—they can read but just don't want to. Others are *struggling* readers who have difficulty decoding the words on the page.

The way to help a reluctant reader (and they are often but not always boys) is to make it easy to read something enjoyable. Don't worry about whether they are reading a comic book or a book about a favorite computer game. Don't worry if they're not reading *books* at all. Place interesting magazine articles wherever they are easy to grab. One mom found that keeping a few comic books close to the microwave almost guaranteed that her child would grab one of them.

If your child is a struggling reader, the problems are probably deep seated and likely to be more challenging to address. You'll know if your child is struggling if they can't seem to remember the sounds that various letters make. They can't recognize simple sight words like *the* or *and* from one day to the next.

Kids struggle for many reasons. They may have attention issues that make it make it hard for them to sit still. They may have learning disabilities that have not yet been diagnosed. They may be starting to read in English when their family speaks another language at home.

The most typical causes for reading problems are outlined in the following textbox. If you think your child has one or more of these issues, you need to talk to the teacher. Discuss what you're seeing at home. Ask to see any reading tests your child may have taken. Then together, come up with a plan to help your child at school and at home.

Most important of all, make reading a positive experience for your child. If you're reading and your child gets frustrated or starts to cry, just stop. You don't want reading to feel like punishment. Keep your eyes on the goal, which is to help your child enjoy reading.

A growth mindset (see Question 73 in Chapter 8) can also be helpful as your child works through their struggles with reading. As you read at home, try to create opportunities for your child to be successful. Take time before they start to read to see if they can figure out what the passage is about. (Look at pictures. Remember what they read yesterday.) That will give them a head start as they begin to read.

After they have finished reading, help them reflect. What strategies did they use when they got stuck on a word? As they see that they are making progress, they will begin to develop a growth mindset: I'm not a good reader *yet*. But I'm improving!

Causes of most reading problems

Lack of phonemic awareness. Ask your child to tell you a word that rhymes with *mat*. Or see how many words they can think of that start with the same sound as *mother*.

Children who can't do these tasks are missing phonemic awareness—the specific ability to focus on and manipulate individual sounds (phonemes) in spoken words. Each word in English is made up of a series of sounds, so *mat* has three phonemes: /m/, /a/, and /t/. There are actually 44 phonemes in English, including some letter combinations like /sh/ and /ng/. Phonemic awareness is the foundation needed for spelling and for recognizing unfamiliar words. It's also one of the best predictors of how well children will learn to read during their first two years of school.

Word games can help kids develop phonemic awareness. Who can come up with the longest list of words that rhyme with *cat*? What other words start with the same sound as the first letter in your child's name?

Decoding. Good readers recognize many familiar words without having to sound them out. And when they do encounter an unfamiliar word, they can usually sound it out. When children struggle with these skills, they end up struggling over every word. It takes them so long to finish a page that they are usually quite frustrated.

Vocabulary. Suppose your child came across this sentence in a book: "David arrived in a flivver." The word *flivver* is pretty easy to sound out—but most kids (and probably most parents) would have no idea what it means. (It's a slang word from the early 20th century that referred to a car.) Understanding not only how to sound out words but also what they mean is a critical reading skill.

Addressing this problem can actually be fun for the entire family. Try to do new things that might seem to have nothing to do with reading. Go on a walk and see how many different types of leaves you can find. Bake a recipe together. Visit a children's museum to see an exhibit. All these experiences will help your child have more knowledge to bring to a reading assignment on an unfamiliar topic.

Fluency. One easy way to tell that a child is struggling with reading is to listen to them read aloud. If they start and stop, and if the reading sounds choppy, they lack the fluency they need to be a successful reader. Kids who find reading to be a laborious chore are, not surprisingly, unwilling to spend much time at it. But when students move into the upper elementary grades, they simply have more reading to do each day.

Look for books that have repeating word patterns and invite your child to join in as you read aloud. (There is nothing quite so jolly as the 15th rendition of *Alexander and the Terrible, Horrible, No Good, Very Bad Day!*) Or find a story your child enjoys and have them read it aloud several times. Can they read to their baby sister? Can they do a call to read it to their grandparents?

Comprehension. By definition, a lot of the reading assignments given to children in school have to do with things they don't already know. But good readers have the ability to decode all the words and then to make connections between what they are reading and what they already know.

After reading, encourage your child to think back over what they just read. Can they retell the story in their own words? Can they retell the story of Little Red Riding Hood from the point of view of the wolf?

Learning disabilities. Some children may have learning disabilities that make reading even more difficult. Children with these disabilities may process information in ways that make it much more of a challenge to read. With assistance from a specially trained teacher, children can learn how their brain best works so they can be successful in school.

If you suspect that your child has any of these reading problems, talk with their teacher. Ask to look at the reading tests your child has taken. Discuss what these tests show about your child's strengths and weaknesses. (And see Question 32 later in this chapter, which outlines how to get your child evaluated.)

Reading challenges will not go away by themselves. But when the school and the parent work together, your child's reading problems can usually be systematically addressed.

27. WHAT DO I NEED TO KNOW ABOUT THE MATH PROGRAM AT MY CHILD'S ELEMENTARY SCHOOL?

If there's a subject that gives parents high anxiety, it's generally math. Speaking just for myself here, I didn't like math. I stopped taking it as soon as I could.

I cheered when Kathleen Turner, playing the role of the time-traveling Peggy Sue in *Peggy Sue Got Married*, talked back to her algebra teacher: "Mr. Snelgrove, I happen to know that in the future I will not have the slightest use for algebra, and I speak from experience."

And then my kid started school, and I found myself right back in the soup. Although no one would ever call me a star math parent, I managed to raise a kid who was not a math-phobe. And who took calculus at the college level.

So here's what I know about what you need to know about math:

Learn what the school is teaching. You need to know what your child is expected to learn at each grade level, at least at a higher level. It's the only way you can know whether your child is learning what they need to. Chapter 2, Question 15 lays out a grade-by-grade set of learning goals that have been curated by the organization Seek Common Ground (SCG).

If your child is not meeting these goals, you may need to talk to the teacher. If your school is not teaching this content at this grade, you may want to find out why. That is the subject for Chapter 9. You may also want to use outside resources to be sure your child is not left behind.

Find other ways to promote math. Talk about situations times when you use math in real life. If you're preparing a recipe, have your child help. And look for examples of where you use math in everyday life, whether it's checking out at the grocery store or figuring out how much paint to buy when you're painting a room in your house.

Ask questions that involve math. Don't be too quick to give the answer. In a TED Talk about math, Dan Finkel, founder of the organization Math for Love, offered a tough truth: "It's not uncommon for students to graduate from high school believing that every math problem can be solved in 30 seconds or less, and if they don't know the answer, they're just not a math person. This is a failure of education. We need to teach kids to be tenacious and courageous, to persevere in the face of difficulty. The only way to teach perseverance is to give students time to think and grapple with real problems."[4]

Play. As Finkel said, "What books are to reading, play is to mathematics. And a home filled with blocks and puzzles and games and play is a home where mathematical thinking can flourish." So whether you're playing board games or card games, make math a game.

Don't pass along your anxiety. Math really is the gatekeeper to college and a good job. So even if you don't love math, try not to pass that feeling on.

28. IT SEEMS LIKE MY CHILD IS SPENDING A LOT OF TIME MEMORIZING THINGS LIKE MATH FACTS AND SIGHT WORDS. IS MEMORIZATION REALLY NECESSARY?

The best way to answer this question is with another question. Say you're in the kitchen and you want to get to the bedroom. Do you think to yourself, "Now I need to pick up my left foot and put it in front of me"? Of course not. You simply start walking, perhaps thinking about what you need to do once you arrive in the bedroom.

Yet for a 15-month-old, making that same trip would require intense concentration. They *would* have to think carefully about where they placed their foot for each step.

Tasks we repeat over and over become automatic. Unless we suffer an injury, we don't need to devote conscious energy to walking once we've mastered the task. Since we can walk without thinking consciously about what we're doing, we can actually (you knew this was coming) walk and chew gum at the same time.

The same thing is true for reading. Most of us glance at the headlines in the newspaper without giving much thought to sounding out the words. Because reading has become automatic, we can think about what the words are *saying*—that there's a flood in South America, or that the voters elected our preferred candidate for mayor.

The ability to do a task without consciously thinking about it is called *automaticity*. And it doesn't happen, well, automatically.

Skills improve with practice until they become automatic. An Olympic swimmer can't dive into the pool and then wonder how to swim the butterfly. They need to focus on where the other swimmers are in the pool. A world-class pianist can't concentrate on which note comes next in a Beethoven piano sonata. Instead, they must concentrate on how to make each note as musical as possible. As we saw in Chapter 1, Question 2, reaching proficiency takes time.

So the goal for important subjects like math and reading is to develop automaticity. Then when your child has to read a challenging social studies assignment, they won't be thinking about sounding out the words. Instead, they'll concentrate on what those words mean, and how this information relates to things they already know.

Math students who don't have to think about the sum of 7 plus 9 are instead freed up to think about the problem itself. And while that is important in grade school, it becomes critical in higher levels of math. It's hard to think about how to solve for x if you can't remember the product of 3 times 6.

What does this mean for you?

- Practice really does make perfect. So while your child is learning to read, be sure they get plenty of practice. Try to set aside at least 15 minutes each day for reading. This should be reading just for fun—so don't worry if they only want to read about sports heroes or computer games. The great cellist Pablo Casals was once asked why he still practiced 5 hours a day at the age of 85. "Because I think I am getting better," he replied.
- Memorizing math facts is critical. Some schools emphasize mastering math facts; others don't. If your school falls into the latter category, you'll have to step in. Make flash cards. Play math games that require quick recall of math facts. Look for computer games that develop automaticity. I was eternally grateful for a math program whose main character cheered and turned cartwheels every single time Sara got a right answer. Every. Single. Time. I, on the other hand, lost interest in whooping it up after about five minutes. She loved the applause, and she learned the math.

29. MY CHILD FORGETS THE THINGS THEY NEED TO TAKE TO AND FROM SCHOOL. HOW DO I HELP MY CHILD TAKE RESPONSIBILITY FOR SCHOOL ASSIGNMENTS AND MATERIALS?

I'm sure there are kids who get back and forth to school every day with all the work and equipment they need. I just never met any of them.

For most families, the process of teaching kids how to get organized about their schoolwork is a long one. Fair warning, it will start out with you feeling (correctly) that you are doing most of the organizing and remembering. But over time, these steps will become habits and you'll be less and less involved.

Most kids are forgetful at least some of the time. They're rushing to catch the bus so they leave their book report in their bedroom. After school, they're *pretty* sure they left their math book at school (they know it is not in their backpack). But maybe they left it at soccer practice?

As a result, mornings in many households are pretty chaotic. Kid 1 is racing around looking for the library book that is due today. Kid 2 has just reminded you that they need a permission slip for the field trip tomorrow (and you're not sure where the permission slip is). You're watching the clock and hoping that the bus will be at least a minute or two late so you don't have to drive everyone to school.

The best way to avoid the morning chaos at your house: Create systems and develop habits. As Chip and Dan Heath said in their book *Switch: How to Change Things When Change Is Hard*, "What looks like a people problem is often a situation problem."[5] So make it as easy as possible for your child and your family by creating a system to keep them organized.

Create a "landing pad." Set up a place where your child puts everything they brought home from school. Help them build the habit of unloading the minute they walk in the door. Use hooks so they have a place to hang their coat. Above it, install a small magnetic whiteboard where you can write notes or attach papers that need to go back to school. Below the hook, have a box or basket for shoes or boots as well as bulky items. "The families I know who are raising independent kids have developed a routine for after school," said Ellingsen. "Coats go on the hook. The backpack goes on the shelf. And the red folder from school goes in the place where all the family mail is kept."

Check the backpack every day. Even with all the electronic communication methods available, schools still rely on backpack mail. You do not want to discover this in November when you clean out the smushed-up papers and old banana peels in your child's book bag, only to discover you have missed parent–teacher conferences and the fall book fair.

Make sure your child has a list of every assignment. Get a brightly colored two-pocket folder that goes back and forth between home and school. Any papers that have to be completed—such as a math worksheet or a social studies map—go in the folder. Many schools also have created websites where teachers post homework assignments online. Or, if your school allows kids to have devices in the classroom, encourage them to take a picture of the homework board in the classroom. They can take a picture of any assignment sheets the teacher hands out as well. It's much harder to lose a digital photo than a piece of paper in the bottom of a stuffed backpack.

Then set up a regular time each day to go through the file folder together. Are there forms you need to sign? Homework they need to complete? This is also the time to look for the misplaced library book so you don't need to make a mad dash through the house as the bus is pulling up.

As you sign each form or your child finishes each homework assignment, the papers go back in the other side of the folder and the bulkier items go back to the landing pad. Then just be sure the folder goes in the backpack and the backpack is at the landing pad before bedtime.

Keep like with like. Make it as easy as possible for your child to find what they need. Organize by subject and by color. Math homework and worksheets go in a red folder or binder. English goes in a green folder or binder. Each day, everything from that class gets put in the right place.

Use natural consequences where you can. We all know that actions have consequences. A child who forgets their hat will have a chilly head. If they don't write their book report, they'll get a lower grade.

Parents always want to step in and protect their child from these consequences. But you need to step back. The longer you do things your child could do, the longer you are postponing the learning experience. So whenever possible, let your child live out the consequences of their actions. It's not neglect, said Julie Lythcott-Haims in *How to Raise an Adult.* "You're not meant to do *nothing* for [your kids]—you're just not meant to do everything."[6]

You may want to alert the teacher. "We're working on responsibility for getting things to school, so I should warn you that Keisha may show up without her homework a few times. I'll try to help her develop good habits at home, but I want you to know what's going on." Odds are, the teacher will be happy to work with you.

Of course there are some times when you can't let your child experience natural consequences. If your child would be in danger, you have to step in. You pull a child from the street rather than letting them experience the natural consequence of getting hit by a car. You should also intervene if failing could cause your child public embarrassment. If every other kid in the school chorus has a white shirt and your child's shirt is hanging on the back of the closet door . . . just take it to school.

It will take time to build these habits. But you'll increase the odds that your child gets to school with the things they need . . . and make your mornings much less stressful!

Another great way to help build responsibility is to let your child start to learn how to do some life skills. For example, even in first grade, your child can be taught to

- mix, stir, and cut with a dull knife;
- make a basic meal, like a sandwich;
- help put the groceries away; and
- wash the dishes.

Your child should also learn how to

- use basic household cleaners safely;
- straighten up the bathroom after using it;
- make their bed without assistance; and
- bathe unsupervised.

30. MY DAUGHTER'S FIFTH-GRADE CLASS HAS DIVIDED INTO CLIQUES. IT'S PAINFUL FOR ME TO WATCH AS HER FORMER FRIENDS NOW EXCLUDE HER. WHAT CAN I DO?

Fifth grade is the start of a rough couple of years for cliques. While it's natural for kids to form groups of friends as early as preschool, it's typically in the upper elementary grades that some of these groups start leaving other kids out on purpose. And while boys do have cliques, they are more common among girls—and the behavior is much more likely to be meaner and more hurtful.

As a parent, it's natural to feel helpless, angry, and nearly as hurt as your child when it happens to them. You want to jump in, to call the other parents, to insist that they take your child back as part of the group.

Don't.

There's very little chance you can change the group's behavior anyway. And even if you *do*, what have you taught your child? Mostly, the lesson they'll learn is that they can't handle things and that you will always be there to rescue them when they get in trouble.

Yes, it hurts to have your child left out. But they *will* get over it. You can help. Talk with them about what's going on. Agree that it sure hurts to be left out. But point out that they are a great person. Right now, a few kids just don't see that.

Help them think about other kids who share their interests. Are there kids on the soccer team they might spend time with? Kids from church? Or perhaps they can do something new, like trying out for a play or signing up for a tae kwon do class.

They could try spending time with just one friend who is now part of the clique. (This may not work, especially if the pull of the clique is very strong. But it's worth a try.)

They may also decide they need to change so they can fit in better. And a lot of people do try a little self-improvement (as anyone who has ever walked through a bookstore can attest). But they need to be clear why they're making the changes—and that they aren't changing for others. Because really, if your daughter who has always loved to read now decides she can't be seen with a book or other girls will make fun of her—are those the girls she wants running her life?

You should probably avoid talking with the teacher about this. However, if the cliquishness turns to bullying, then you will have to step in. There is more about this, particularly when the bullying goes online, in Question 41 in Chapter 5.

Meanwhile, help your child take the long view. Things change. Friendships grow and fade away. The most important thing they can do is to make friends they can have fun with and talk to. The best way to find those friends is to be that kind of person. And that will last a lot longer than any fifth-grade clique.

31. DO I NEED TO
GO TO PARENT–TEACHER CONFERENCES?

Once or twice a year, most schools invite parents in for a parent–teacher conference. So you dutifully troop off to school, sit in a little chair, and spend a harried 15 or 20 minutes talking with your child's teacher.

The process is, frankly, not always satisfying for *either* parents or teachers. Parents who have conscientiously developed a list of questions for the teacher often find that there isn't time to get the answers they want. Teachers who want to go over a child's work with parents find that they have to cut short a promising conversation because there's another parent waiting in the hall.

So the obvious question parents ask is whether they should bother to go to the parent–teacher conference at all. And if they should, what can they do to make it more productive?

The answer to the first question is yes. Attending the parent–teacher conference, even it isn't a perfect way to find out everything you need to know about how your child is doing in school, still matters. If you want to develop two-way communication between the school and your family, a parent–teacher conference is one important step.

Before the conference, spend a few minutes talking with your child. Find out what *they* would like you to discuss. Ask them what the teacher might say. What does your child like, or not like, this year in school?

Then make your own list of questions. Here are some to get you started:

- What will be covered in this grade or subject this year?
- What are your expectations for homework?
- Has my child missed any assignments?
- How are their work habits? Does my child use time well?
- Are they reading at the level you would expect for this grade?
- Are they doing math at the level you would expect for this grade?
- Do they qualify for any special programs (e.g., gifted and talented, English as a second language, or special education)?

If there's anything special you think the teacher needs to know, the conference is a good time to share that. This might include your child's favorite subjects, outside interests, and any medical or health needs. Also, if there's anything going on at home that might affect schoolwork, let the teacher know.

32. MY FOURTH GRADER IS STRUGGLING IN SCHOOL. I THINK THEY MAY HAVE A LEARNING DISABILITY. SHOULD I ASK FOR A MEETING WITH THE TEACHER?

Yes. Good teachers have always tried to adjust their teaching to meet the needs of students who are having trouble keeping up with the rest of the class. That means you need to tell the teacher what you're seeing at home.

However, before you schedule that meeting, you should know a little bit about what you and your child have a legal right to expect. Since 1975, the federal government has had a law protecting the educational needs of children with disabilities. The current version of that law, the Individuals With Disabilities Education Act, is usually just called IDEA.

Under IDEA, parents have a right to request an evaluation of their child's learning progress. While the school does not have to do a full evaluation, they are required at least to review your child's educational status and determine whether they are experiencing significant learning difficulties.

Ideally, you'll make notes and look for examples of your concerns about your child's learning. You can also share things the teacher would not know: Your child, who used to look forward to school, now asks to stay home every day. Each day's homework session ends with your child in tears. You asked your child to read aloud and they struggled to sound out every word. The National Center for Learning Disabilities has a comprehensive list of things that might indicate that a child has a learning disability (https://www.ncld .org/wp-content/uploads/2014/11/IDEA-Parent-Guide.pdf).

The teacher may also share observations with you. Trust the instinct of a veteran teacher, but remember that you always know your child best. Perhaps the teacher will start by suggesting some new approaches to helping your child learn. That may be a positive approach, but you do need to insist on regular monitoring and reporting on what is being tried and how it's working.

You have a right to request a formal evaluation. It should be in writing, and you should keep a copy. One of the things to know about special education is that record keeping is critical. Use the sample letter at the end of this chapter and personalize it for your child.

Remember that during this entire process, you have the right to see your child's educational records, to ask for copies you may keep, and to have the records explained to you by school staff. If the records include information that you know is inaccurate or misleading, you can ask that the records be changed. If that request is denied, you have the right to a hearing so you can challenge the information.

The process of determining that a child qualifies for special education services and the ongoing work that parents have to make sure the school is meeting their child's needs are extensive. Most parents find that they come to rely on other parents of children with disabilities for support as they move through a process that is at best complicated and at times overwhelming.

You may also want to reach out to your state or region's Parent Center. There are 100 such centers across the nation, and they can provide information and training in how you can be a better advocate for your child. Here's where you can find the list by state: https://www.parentcenterhub .org/find-your-center/.

In many cases, children who are significantly behind their classmates may have a learning disability. But you should also be aware that there can be other reasons why a child is struggling:

- A physical condition, such as poor vision or hearing, may interfere with your child's ability to learn.

- Your child may have cultural or language barriers that make learning in class difficult.
- Your child might never have been taught the academic content that the teacher is now building on.
- The way the school teaches basic skills such as reading may not be effective for every child.

Letter requesting a special education evaluation

Send this letter to the principal, inserting your information and situation.

Dear Dr. Smith,

I am writing to you because my child Jessica (BIRTH DATE) is experiencing problems in school. I believe she needs to be evaluated to determine whether she may need special education services.

Jessica's test scores show that she is reading on the second-grade level (SPECIFIC SCORE). She reads aloud very slowly and often confuses words when she is reading. As a result, she cannot read many of the assignments in science and history by herself.

Her teacher, Ms. Jackson, reports that while Jessica tries hard, she often substitutes or leaves out words while she is reading. She guesses at unfamiliar words because she has difficulty linking letters with sounds. (OTHER INFORMATION)

As each day goes by, Jessica is falling further and further behind her classmates and what is expected of fourth graders. As a result, I believe it is critical that Jessica be evaluated.

I understand that you will send me a plan for how the evaluation will proceed, and which tests you may give to Jessica. Once I have given you my approval for the evaluation, may I also request that you let me know when you have scheduled the evaluation?

I would appreciate other information you think may be helpful to me. I would especially appreciate information on timelines, deadlines, and information you may request of me as we move through this process.

I appreciate your help. I know we all want Jessica to be successful in school.

Very sincerely,

YOUR NAME

5

QUESTIONS PARENTS SHOULD ASK ABOUT MIDDLE SCHOOL

You can't say everything you think.

—Good advice for a middle schooler
from a former middle school teacher

"Parents think that the transition to high school will be tough," said Stacey Finkel, who has a son in middle school and another in high school. "And it is. But I think the transition to middle school is much more of a challenge."

From the elementary school where they knew everyone and were the social leaders, students move to a middle school that is usually much larger. They focus more on peers than parents and may experiment with things like clothing and hair. But some of their elementary school friends may now go to a different school. Some of their friends may suddenly decide they are *not* friends.

In middle school, students have to learn an entirely new way to do school. They have more teachers—moving from one or two to six, seven, or even eight. Each one of those teachers probably expects more than an elementary school teacher. Assignments are longer. Teachers don't hover to make sure students get them done on time. Academic expectations are typically higher.

And then, every day, they have to navigate a complex maze of crowded hallways *and* a locker with a combination lock that might have been devised by a cryptographer. No wonder middle school kids feel so confused.

Add into this entire mix the hormonal and physical changes that come during the middle school years—when kids are often more mature physically than they are emotionally—and you have a pretty formidable set of challenges for any kid to maneuver. So it's no wonder that parents have a lot of questions as they send their young teen off to middle school.

In this book, "middle school" includes the ages between 11 and 14, which in most schools means Grades 6, 7, and 8. These grades are seen as a transition between elementary school and high school.

My sister Sue taught middle school band for 37 years. She said that kids this age are a study in contrasts. They are "part little kid, part adult." They alternate between being completely oblivious to their surroundings and being hyperfocused. And they say whatever is on their minds.

One day in the middle of a lesson, and seemingly out of nowhere, a girl looked down at Sue's feet and said, "Brown shoes and black socks. Major fashion error."

It was that quality that led her to decide that the most important lesson she could teach middle school students was this: "You can't say everything you think." That's a good lesson for parents to teach as well.

And, she said, master these two phrases, which will very likely defuse at least a few battles: "Oh, well," and "Not today."

"Everybody else is doing it."

"Oh, well."

"Can I get a tattoo?"

"Not today."

Note that in either case, you haven't actually had to say no. But you've said no for now, and with middle schoolers that may be the best you can hope for.

Besides, "Will I live through this?" there are some other key questions parents of middle schoolers should ask.

33. MY SON HAS NEVER HAD TO DO MUCH FOR HIMSELF. I KNOW THAT HAS TO CHANGE IN MIDDLE SCHOOL. WHAT SHOULD I DO TO GET HIM TO TAKE ON MORE RESPONSIBILITY?

When children start elementary school, there are a lot of things they can't do for themselves. So their parents do it for them. And somehow, as they move up through the grades, those responsibilities never change.

Kids are not stupid—if they figure out that they can go through their life without having to worry about packing a school lunch or making sure they have clean underwear, they're only too happy to let someone else take on those chores.

The start of middle school is a good time to rethink what you are doing for your child. You should make the transition to having them assume as much responsibility as possible. Think of this as starting the glide path to prepare your child for adult life.

You're moving to a new role as a parent. You're shifting from becoming the doer to becoming the coach.

Question 5 in Chapter 1 talks about *helicopter* and *bulldozer* parents— those who hover over their kids full-time or those who simply plow ahead to clear a path. As Julie Lythcott-Haims said in *How to Raise an Adult*, many parents have created a new role for themselves in their teen's life— "a position that's partly personal assistant and partly like the role high-end publicists play in the lives of some Hollywood stars: observer, handler, and, often, go-between."[1]

Middle school is a good time for a reset. Even if you were a helicopter parent before, now's the time to back off. Let your young teen develop what kids now call their *adulting* skills.

It may be messy at first. Actually, it's almost certain to be messy at least some of the time. But young teens who learn how to take responsibility for their own well-being will also be developing the ability to handle other challenges that life throws at them.

Start each school year by turning over responsibility for one thing and for loosening at least one rule. Make a list of the things you have done for your teen. Sit with them and talk through all the ways they can take on those tasks.

Did you wake them up in the morning? They need an alarm clock that they have to get out of bed to turn off. (For all kinds of reasons, using a smartphone as an alarm clock is generally a bad idea. Instead of getting out of bed to get ready for school, teens will instantly start checking social media and probably miss the bus.)

Did you pack their lunch? They can take on that chore. As a plus, they can decide what they really want to eat. And when they move into the nearly inevitable vegetarian or vegan period that most kids go through (and for some, it becomes a permanent lifestyle change), they can be the ones to remember to add peanut butter or chickpeas to the shopping list.

There's no reason that a middle schooler can't be responsible for their own laundry. Yes, there may be a few disasters—a college friend had a few embarrassing athletic practices wearing the workout clothes he hadn't realized would turn pink if he threw his red football jersey into the load of whites. It was, he said, a mistake he needed to make only once.

You'll need to teach them each of these tasks, breaking them down (like a good coach) step by step. You'll have to expect some mishaps. And you'll probably need to offer some sort of trade-off (or trade-up). You might increase your child's allowance as you are turning over laundry responsibilities.

But when they don't do everything the way you would—and they won't—don't be critical. They're going to learn, and perhaps the hard way, that if you don't wash your favorite T shirt, you can't wear it to school the next day. They'll be more likely to remember the next time they want to put off doing the laundry. Remind them that, as author Anne Lamott said, "It's good to do uncomfortable things. It's weight training for life." (They will not appreciate this now. In fact, they will likely roll their eyes. But they will repeat it to their own middle schoolers eventually.) All this is how middle schoolers learn how to solve their own problems. And that's something to celebrate.

34. MY SON WAS NEVER MR. POPULARITY, BUT HE DID HAVE SOME GOOD FRIENDS IN ELEMENTARY SCHOOL. NOW THEY'RE AT OTHER SCHOOLS OR HANGING OUT WITH OTHER KIDS. HOW CAN I HELP HIM MAKE NEW FRIENDS?

Middle school is a time when friendships change. Because friendships are such a critical part of middle school, it can be painful to watch as your young teen adjusts to this new reality.

One of the bad things about middle school is that there are a lot of kids your teen has never met. But that can also turn out to be one of the best things about middle school, since there are always new and different people to interact with.

Friendships are typically forged through shared interests, whether it is playing on the same team or playing the same quirky computer game. Can you help your teen think about where people who share their interests might be found? If they are a sports lover who didn't make the team, could they find another sport to try, whether it's archery or Ultimate Frisbee?

Remember that all friendships don't have to be based at the school. A theater lover might try out for a community theater and make some new friends. Or encourage a young teen to look for a school activity that was not offered in elementary school. Many middle and high schools publish newspapers, which need photographers, layout artists, and editors in addition to writers. There may be a computer club where they can learn a new skill.

And while we are talking about making friends, this is as good a time as any to introduce a sensitive issue. Middle schoolers, particularly middle school boys, need to wear deodorant. Every day. This is not negotiable.

If making new friends seems daunting, don't let them get discouraged. If they have made friends before, they can make friends again.

35. MY MIDDLE SCHOOLER NEVER SEEMS TO GET THEIR HOMEWORK DONE ON TIME, SO THEY DON'T GET ENOUGH SLEEP AND START THE NEXT DAY IN A BIG RUSH. HOW CAN I HELP?

"Stuff counts. Suddenly, everything is real." That was the biggest change that Paige Kowalski, mother of two adolescent boys, noticed when they made the transition from elementary school to middle school.

In retrospect, she said, when she thinks about elementary school, "I have '70s music in my head—it's sweet and all sunshine." Then in middle school, things take a turn. That transition, she said, is "jarring."

Kids have more teachers. Instead of the one teacher who knew them and nurtured them, they have five, six, or even seven. And each of them expects students to do more on their own. Students have regular homework in most classes, and they might have big projects due on the same day. Learning to be responsible for this homework, and for getting assignments completed on time, is one of the most significant responsibilities they'll have in school.

By the time teens reach the middle grades, they are sometimes less motivated to do well in school. And they are sometimes frustrated by homework that they can't see connecting in any way to their life. ("Why do we need to learn this anyway?" is perhaps the number-one homework question asked of middle school teachers.)

All that means is that in too many cases, middle schoolers are likely to end up starting their history paper an hour after they needed to be in bed. They need to learn how to manage their time effectively. And in many schools, time management is not something that is explicitly taught.

But they can't manage time until they know what they need to do with it. So middle schoolers need to start with a complete listing of everything they have to do in every class. Find a calendar or a personal planner that will work for your child. There are some apps that can be helpful, but a big calendar with lots of room for writing things in will work just as well. The key to any planner is what information is *in* it. Have your teen write down the date of any upcoming tests, papers, or projects. That will help them plan backward so they are sure to get it done.

There's nothing like the power of a daily to-do list. Each day, after adding anything new to their calendar, have them write down the things that have to be done:

- go to soccer practice;
- walk the dog;
- study for Spanish test Friday (30 minutes);
- finish math worksheet; and
- read science assignment and answer the questions at the end.

Seeing everything in writing will also help them figure out when to do what. If science is their toughest subject, they should start their homework session with that. If math comes easier, they can do the worksheet at the end.

Note that this list includes some time spent studying for a test that is several days off. Cramming is not an effective strategy for learning anything. Breaking studying down into several shorter periods spread over several days will be more likely to produce a positive result! (For more on how to study for a test, see Question 74 in Chapter 8.)

There are more large projects in middle school, projects that can create anxiety for students who are new to the process. It will seem less overwhelming and will be less likely to be left until the last minute if it's done in chunks, each with its own deadline. This will create smaller, manageable subtasks out of the larger, more daunting tasks.

And what if your middle schooler really is spending hours and hours on homework? If you've determined that they are doing their work and not checking out their social media accounts, that could be a signal that there's something wrong. They may need extra help in a class. They could even need tutoring. (More on that in Question 48, Chapter 6.)

One of the ways you can help is by connecting what your teen learns in school to what they want to do later in life. A study of more than 50,000 students done by the Harvard Graduate School of Education found that relating academic achievement to life's later goals is one of the most effective thing parents can do to help their teens.[2]

On the other hand, the study shows that a parent's direct involvement in homework is actually not very effective—and sometimes counterproductive. (You may find this a huge relief if your teen's math classes have moved beyond your ability to help anyway.) Teens reported that direct parent involvement is more likely to be seen as interference. It can also be confusing if parents don't use the same strategies as their teachers.

Here are some other specific strategies for math homework:

- Don't project your own math anxiety. Follow the advice given to doctors: First, do no harm. So get your teen to talk about math class. Ask what they are learning. You may find that you learn something yourself!
- If your teen is stuck on a problem, have them talk through what they know and what they've already done. If they are trying to solve a word problem, have them read it aloud. Can they draw a picture or a diagram of the problem? Then figure out what they are actually being asked to solve, which is likely to be the last question in the problem. ("When will the two trains meet?") What math operations are needed—addition, subtraction, multiplication, or division? Now see if your teen can solve the problem.
- Look for online help. There are lots of resources that break down math skills and teach them in engaging ways. Many teachers swear by the Khan Academy (khanacademy.org), but there are other content providers. At Back to School Night, ask the math teacher for recommendations.

So think of this book as your homework pass. Don't feel that you need to get in there and help your kid solve for x. Instead, remind them how math is likely to help them in the future.

36. MY MIDDLE SCHOOLER HAS THE OPTION OF TAKING ALGEBRA IN EIGHTH GRADE OR IN NINTH. WHICH IS BEST?

When Michael Pollan, author of *The Omnivore's Dilemma*, was asked if he could summarize everything he'd learned about healthy nutrition, he summed up his advice in three sentences: "Eat food. Not too much. Mostly plants."

My advice on how to prepare a middle schooler for college is equally simple: "Take math. All you can. Especially early algebra."

In a report called *Building Blocks of Success*, the nonprofit organization Achieve noted, "Advanced high school math is a ticket to college access."[3] That building blocks analogy is important. Math, more than almost any other subject, builds on what students have already learned. You have to be able to count to 100 before you can add and subtract numbers within 100. You have to know how to divide whole numbers before you can work with fractions.

Algebra I is a foundation class. Without it, students close the door on other advanced-level courses. And the clock is ticking. Algebra II (which you obviously can't take until you've completed Algebra I) is a requirement for physics, and if a student doesn't complete Algebra II until junior or senior year, physics or an Advanced Placement science class will be impossible. No wonder Achieve found that students who have completed math classes at least through Algebra II say they feel prepared for college.

Northwestern University professor James Rosenbaum noted that the more math students take in high school, the greater their chance of earning a college degree. While 79.8% of students whose highest high school math class is calculus earn a college degree, the odds of graduating drop as the level of the last math class goes down. For students whose last high school math class was precalculus, 74.3% will graduate with a degree. But if Algebra I is their last class, only 7.8% will achieve a college degree.[4]

Even if your teen is not a math whiz, algebra can help. One Florida study found that students who had taken Algebra II in high school were less likely to have to take a remedial (as in, noncredit) math class in college. That was true even if they got a D in the class.[5]

Parents play a big role in whether their child takes advanced math classes. You may worry that you do not remember the math you took in high school. You may not have *taken* much math in high school. And luckily there's other research, discussed in the previous question, that says parents do not actually have to *know* the math. Nor do they have to be able to help with the substance of what is being taught. But talking about the importance of taking these higher-level classes and helping your young teen see how they can open doors seem to make the biggest difference.

A word of caution for parents of Black and Brown students: You may need to push a little to get your child on this track to success. Data collected by the U.S. Office of Civil Rights noted significant racial disparities in enrolling in higher-level math. The data, based on the 2015–2016 Civil Rights Data Collection survey of U.S. public schools revealed the following:

- Black students make up 17% of the overall eighth-grade enrollment but only 11% of those enrolled in Algebra 1.
- Latino students made up 25% of the overall enrollment but only 18% of those taking Algebra 1.
- Eighty-five percent of white students passed Algebra 1 in eighth grade, while only 65% of Black students did. Asian and Latino students were nearly tied, at 74% and 72%, respectively.[6]

You may find that your school does not offer the option to take Algebra I in middle school—schools that enroll high numbers of students of color far too frequently do not offer the courses that will ensure that students are prepared for college. You can investigate other options for your child—perhaps they can take Algebra I at the high school during their eighth-grade year. Or you can look at the option of taking the course online, perhaps through a local community college.

Of course, if the school is denying this opportunity to all students, it may be time to change the school policy. There's much more on how you can do that in Chapter 9.

37. MY MIDDLE SCHOOLER STRUGGLES WHEN READING TEXTBOOKS IN SUBJECTS LIKE HISTORY OR SCIENCE. WHY IS IT SO HARD FOR TEENS TO READ AND REMEMBER?

For a long time, we thought that learning to read was like getting a permanent tooth—you did it once and it was done. But we now know that even students who are good readers may not know how to read their science, math, or history texts. A position statement by the National Council of Teachers of English explained it this way: "Reading is not a technical skill acquired once and for all in the primary grades, but rather a developmental process throughout the reader's life."[7]

Reading what is known as *informational text*—including textbooks—is a real challenge. It requires skills that are different from reading a newspaper, a magazine story, or a novel. If you read a math book the same way you read a novel, you are not likely to learn everything you need to. And the skills and strategies that work for reading science are not the same as those needed for reading history or math. So in addition to learning the content in each of these subjects, students need to learn the best way to read for meaning in each discipline.

And while most middle and high school teachers are experts on topics like Reconstruction or the linear functions, they do not always have a lot of training in how to teach reading. So their students are often left to figure things out for themselves.

Here are some suggestions that will give middle and high school students a head start as they tackle challenging texts:

- Don't go into a reading assignment cold. Preview the reading assignment by looking it over first. Identify key ideas. Look at pictures and read the caption. In history books, some of the most important information can be presented through photos and captions. In science books, charts may contain vital information. Read chapter headings and words in bold type. They offer an idea of what the chapter is about.
- Think about everything they already know about the topic. Perhaps they haven't studied the Battle of Gettysburg, but they have already learned about the Civil War. What was happening in July of 1863? That will help them get prepared for new text.
- Write some questions that may be answered in the reading assignment. If they have trouble thinking of questions, turn to the end of the chapter and see if there are review questions.
- Identify a knowledge goal for the reading. "By the time I finish this chapter, I will know more about how scientists use the scientific method to test a hypothesis."
- Learn the vocabulary. Each subject your teen studies in school has its own vocabulary. Words often have a specialized meaning in a particular discipline.
- Read everything on the page. In science, the symbols and diagrams are at least as important as the words. In a history book, a chart may tell an important story. As your teen finds answers to questions, check them off their list. If he has not found answers to all his questions, go back to reread.
- Summarize. Can your teen restate, in their own words, what they just read? If they can, then they are finished with their reading. If they can't, they need to go back through each of the steps again.

- Help your teen see the link between effort and achievement. Those who read the assignment carefully, all the way to the end, who take notes, and who answer the questions at the end of the assignment are more likely to remember what they have read. There's a rubric that can help make this link in Question 73, Chapter 8.

38. MY MIDDLE SCHOOLER WENT FROM HAVING ONE TEACHER TO HAVING SIX. HOW DO I STAY ON TOP OF WHAT'S REQUIRED FOR SO MANY CLASSES?

Many parents believe that once their kids get to middle school, they don't have a role to play. But the truth is that middle school students both want and need parents involved. That involvement will have a different look. Middle schools seldom have room mothers. Middle schoolers don't want you to show up in their homeroom delivering their forgotten science homework (although they'd like you to get it to them as long as their friends don't see the handoff).

Still, you need to stay in touch. Here are some ways you can know what's going on in middle school without humiliating your middle schooler.

Use technology. If you are expecting your middle schooler to bring home a flyer or a newsletter from the school, let me disabuse you of that notion. Middle school students just won't do that.

That's where technology can step in. First, check out the school's web page. It contains a wealth of information you need to know, including the days school will be closed for a teacher workshop or the email addresses of teachers and school staff.

Then check to see whether any teachers have their own web page or portal. These can provide a wealth of information as well, including home-work assignments and the dates for tests and quizzes. Some portals also give you a virtual look into the teacher's gradebook so you can see whether homework assignments have been turned in.

Check the school's policies, including the rules about discipline. Either on the website or in that big packet of material the school will send home on the first day of school, you should find the rules and regulations that outline expected behavior for students. (It may be called the student handbook or the student code of conduct.)

This is where you'll find the rules about attendance, cheating, fighting, and drugs. You will also find the school's policies on bullying, including how to report bullying or the consequences for bullies.

You and your middle schooler should talk about these rules. Let them know that you will support the school's consequences if they break the rules.

Meet teachers in person when you can. There are usually two opportunities to meet with middle school teachers: Back to School Night and parent–teacher conferences. If it's at all possible, try to attend both.

Back to School Night is typically held very early in the school year. Parents follow their child's schedule, spending perhaps 10 minutes in each class. Obviously it's not the time for you to discuss any specific concerns, but you will get a sense of how long a walk it is to get from history class to PE, learn that the math teacher assigns homework every weeknight but not on weekends, and realize that the books they are going to read in English class include a couple of your favorites.

Parent–teacher conferences at the middle school level can be a scheduling challenge, but they're worth the effort. You'll likely move from room to room, and you'll have less time with each teacher. But you can make sure homework is being turned in. You can share information about strengths and weaknesses. And if there is one class where your child is really struggling, you can ask for a follow-up, longer conference.

You might also consider taking your child with you to the conference. (Check with the teacher to see if it's allowed.) A growing number of schools find that having students sit with parents during conferences opens up honest conversations.

These student-led conferences are most successful if students have time to prepare first. They should select samples of their work that they want their parents to see. They should also be prepared to talk about their goals for the school year.

Of course, there are times when students should not be a part of a conference. If a teacher has a serious concern about a child's in-class behavior, for example, the child should probably not be present for the initial conference. If a teacher or parent believes that the student may have a learning problem, they might speak more freely if the student is not in the room. For these reasons, some schools reserve the last 5 minutes of a conference for a parent-to-teacher conversation, with the child absent from the room.

But in many other cases, parents will find that they learn more from the conference if their child is present. Talk with your child's teacher. Ask if they have considered student-led conferences.

If the school does not want to adopt this idea, you can still do it at home. Following the conference, ask your child to create their own portfolio of work. Have them go through the folder and talk about the assignments. Ask them to reflect on what they have learned. You could also try a home conference if you are unable to attend parent–teacher conferences at school.

39. HOW CAN I HELP MY MIDDLE SCHOOLER HANDLE PEER PRESSURE?

Peer pressure doesn't start in middle school, as any parent who has been hounded into buying the latest PlayStation (because everybody else has one) can confirm. But by the time children start middle school, relationships with peers are even more important.

Teens take their first steps toward independence by establishing close relationships with their peer group. Peers help teens learn about friendship, trust, and the importance of give-and-take in a relationship. With peers, teens learn social skills that will help them throughout their adult lives.

But peers can also exert negative peer pressure. Teens often say they use alcohol or drugs because "everybody's doing it." Even practices like eating disorders can be affected by a teen's friends.[8]

Peer groups play an important role in your teen's development, and it's not all bad. As teens grow up, one of their most important tasks is to separate from their parents and develop their own identity. But that's a long and scary journey, so peers provide a safe stopping point along the way. Laurence Steinberg, a psychology professor at Temple University, said in his book *Adolescence* that a young teen's *level* of conformity doesn't really change much. But as they move from childhood into adolescence, they are more likely to conform to their peers than their parents.[9]

That doesn't mean your influence over your teen disappears as they move into middle school. On some big issues—your core values, for example, or the importance of education in your family—you still play an outsize influence in their beliefs and behavior.

Peers have a particularly large influence on your teen's achievement in school. An article in *Slate* magazine examined research on this topic. The article's author, Ray Fisman, summarized a key finding: "[B]eing surrounded by underachieving classmates has a negative effect on girls *and* boys—both genders feel pressure to conform to the lower standards of their peers. But the studies also show that girls are more sensitive than boys to the presence of *high*-achieving peers. Surround a girl with diligent classmates, and her performance will improve."[10]

So encourage your middle schooler to find peers who share positive values. Try to get to know your child's friends. Can you encourage them to invite people over to hang out on the weekend? Absolutely. For the price of a few pizzas or a pay-per-view movie, you can learn more about the people who are so influential in their life. (No, you cannot hang out with the group. Yes, you can come in occasionally to make sure there's enough food. And if there are teenage boys in the house, there will never be enough food.)

Volunteer to drive an extra carpool (it's amazing what you can learn if you keep absolutely silent while middle schoolers talk in the back seat). And when you do, turn off all the electronics, said parent Janet Soller. "Every device in the car has to be turned off."

Don't make your child feel guilty for wanting to spend time with friends—it's an important part of middle school development. As Soller said, "Get those kids in the kitchen and give them a snack. You'd be amazed at what you'll learn."

There's a lot to say for school bands, as you'll read in Chapter 6. In many high schools, band is where you'll find the kids who are taking advanced classes and getting good grades.

As my sister has said, you pick your battles. While middle school students are "really screaming for limits," they will also push back on every limit you impose. So her advice is to decide where you want to draw your line in the sand. Give in on pink bangs, hold firm on limits on social media, for example.

In order to do that, it's critical that you keep talking and listening to your middle schooler. Your goal is not for them to make smart choices because *you* want them to, but because *they* want to. If you see a TV show about a teen facing a tough choice, talk about it later. "What would you have done?" Your willingness to listen and not lecture will show your child you respect their opinions.

40. MY MIDDLE SCHOOLER WANTS A CELL PHONE. WHAT ARE SOME REASONABLE RULES FOR CELL PHONE USE IN MIDDLE SCHOOL?

Middle school does seem to be the time when most kids end up with a cell phone, although some have probably been whining for one since they were in the third grade. A 2019 survey by Common Sense Media found that just over half of children in the United States—53%—own a smartphone by the age of 11, and 69% own one by age 12.[11]

Getting a cell phone is a big step and one your family should not take lightly. Before you head down to the cellular store, be sure you set up some clear boundaries and expectations for responsible use.

Encourage (actually, enforce) balance. Media use only increases as kids get older, so make sure you're actively protecting your kid's homework time, downtime, and family time from the start. Create times and places that are screen-free (family mealtimes, homework time, and your teen's bedroom are definitely on that list).

Model healthy phone use. You can preach all you want about responsible phone use, but if you are always on your own device, that's the lesson your middle schooler will learn. So be very visible as you turn off your phone for family time. Create a family charging station that is not in *anyone's* bedroom and insist that phones go there at night.

Be online together when you can. Look for a game the two of you can play. Ask your middle schooler to show you a few YouTube videos they enjoy. You can help limit inappropriate content by signing up for an ad-free, paid membership so you can have some say in what your kid sees.

Remind your middle schooler that cell phone use is a privilege. Agree in advance that you will know the device password and that you will occasionally check the phone without advance warning. Look through the apps and social media messages occasionally, especially in the beginning. Check the call and text/chat records—if you see a name or number you don't recognize, find out who they're talking to. If you find out that they are using their phone to bully someone, they lose phone access—period. If you find out that they are accessing inappropriate sites, same rule.

Maintain appropriate boundaries. While the Varsity Blues parents got all the public notoriety, most parents, frankly, don't have an extra half a million dollars lying around to engage in this kind of helicopter parenting. But they can shell out for a cell phone, and by middle school, most kids will have one. Some researchers have called it "the world's longest umbilical cord."[12]

There's nothing wrong with setting up some regular check-ins when your middle schooler is away from home. But if you are one of the 16% of parents who install GPS tracking on your teen's phone (according to the Pew Research Center),[13] you probably need to back off. Otherwise, the only lesson you are teaching is that they can't keep themselves safe without your direct, daily involvement.

41. I'M PRETTY SURE MY DAUGHTER IS BEING CYBERBULLIED. SHE WON'T TALK ABOUT IT, BUT SHE'S WITHDRAWN AND SAD. WHAT CAN PARENTS DO?

There have always been bullies in schools, as anyone who ever read *Tom Brown's Schooldays* can attest. And middle school is often a place where bullying can flourish. Part of the process of fitting *in* is shutting others *out*.

Cyberbullying is widespread. A Pew Research Center survey finds that 59% of U.S. teens have personally experienced some abusive online behavior.[14]

In *Teach Your Children Well*, Madeline Levine said that bullying is now a "normative middle school experience." She added that "it appears that cyberbullying has even more negative consequences for its victims than traditional physical bullying, probably because of the profound sense of helplessness and isolation it engenders."[15] In the past, the bullying ended when the student left the school grounds. Today, cyberbullies can follow teens 24 hours a day, 7 days a week.

The consequences can be severe. Teens who are being bullied may try to avoid going to school. Their grades are likely to suffer. They can withdraw from family and friends. One 2018 study found that young adults (those under 25) who were cyberbullied were twice as likely to commit suicide or harm themselves in other ways.[16]

So what's a parent to do? First, understand that most teens do want parents to talk about cyberbullying. They generally give parents high marks on what they are doing to help.[17]

Open up the topic if your teen doesn't bring it up. Look for a story or a TV show about cyberbullying. Ask if your teen has seen examples in their school. Ask what advice they would give to someone who has been the victim of cyberbullying. That's the time to add, "And I hope you'd talk to us about it. That's what parents are for. Even if we can't fix the problem, we can be there with you."

This is a good time to review and perhaps revise your family's rules about online engagement. Be sure your teen understands family rules about things like forwarding embarrassing or hurtful pictures or videos about another person, using anonymous screen names to hide the identity of someone who is being an online bully, or using language that is abusive.

The school needs to be made aware of the issue. While schools can't prevent bullying, whether online or in person, it is reasonable to expect that the school will take action to reduce bullying. The school can ensure that their school policies are up to date and that they are reporting incidents of bullying to the state or federal government as required. They can, and should, encourage tolerance and respect for everyone in the school community. They should ensure that their code of conduct specifically spells out cyberbullying as being against the school rules.

However, to do this, students and parents need to be encouraged to report incidents of bullying on and off the school campus. That can be tough. Kids who report bullying to the authorities are often afraid they will be ostracized even more.

Help your teen find someone at the school they trust. It may be a counselor, a favorite teacher, or a coach. Make an appointment to talk with them. Before they go in, they should keep evidence of what they are experiencing. Save and print screenshots, emails, and text messages. Keep a log of the dates, times, and descriptions of when cyberbullying has occurred.

This kind of active approach will make a bullied teen feel like they are taking back some control of their life. It will also make it much harder for the school to dismiss the issue as "just some harmless prank."

Encourage the school to bring in speakers on cyberbullying for both students and parents. Read the school's behavior code and see if there are ways to strengthen it around bullying issues.

At home, help your teen learn how to block bullies on their device. Report cyberbullying to the social media site so they can take action. Every site has developed terms of service (basically, the right and responsibilities of users). There are no federal laws against bullying, but there is a government website (https://www.stopbullying.gov/resources/laws) that contains links to the state laws governing this behavior.

That's another reason families should keep cell phones out of the bedroom at night. (Put the charging station anywhere else.) You can say it's because phones interfere with sleep (which is true). But you also need to limit the hours your child is exposed to the bullying.

Since research now shows that the bullied often try to turn the tables, understand that there's a pretty clear likelihood that if your teen is being bullied, they may also be bullying someone else.[18] If you find out your teen is engaging in bullying, take steps immediately to stop it. If necessary, restrict your teen's access to devices, at least for a while.

42. MY MIDDLE SCHOOLER IS HAVING TROUBLE IN SEVERAL CLASSES. SHOULD I TALK TO THE COUNSELOR?

In elementary school, you at least knew who to contact if your child was having a problem in class. But now you may have trouble even remembering the names of all your middle schooler's teachers. ("Is Ms. Garcia math? Or is she history?")

So here's a good rule of thumb: If there's a problem in one class, reach out to that teacher. But if the problems are in more than one class, you should make an appointment with the counselor.

Counselors can be a great resource for both parents and students in the middle grades. They can often work with you to solve small problems before they get to be big problems.

You might not recall any contact with your middle school counselor. But today, parents should talk to counselors if they have questions in any of three areas: academic, career, and personal or social.

In the academic area, it will be the school counselor who works with your middle schooler to help develop a schedule. Your job is to be sure your child is taking the classes they need to keep their options open in the future. Ask whether they're taking the math, science, and other classes that will help them get ready for college or a career.

Eleanor Saslaw, who served as a guidance counselor and guidance director for nearly three decades in Fairfax County, Virginia, said that counselors sometimes can help parents see their child in a new way. "For parents who have an automatic reaction to their child's future path, the counselor can help them appreciate their child's personal strengths and weaknesses," she said.

Be sure the counselor knows about your teen's future goals. You do not want your teen to discover as a high school senior that they can't apply to the college of their dreams because they have only taken three years of a foreign language and the college requires four.

Counselors are also helpful when students are thinking about possible careers. In a growing number of states, students and families develop a specific career plan. But even if your state does not require that, you can work with the counselor to explore options and then discuss the education that will prepare a student for that career.

Counselors can also help students with social or emotional problems. A student who is being bullied, for example, should talk with the counselor. So should a student who knows that something's just not right, even if they don't know quite what that something is.

A counselor isn't a therapist, but the counselor could suggest after talking with a student that they could be helped by an outside therapist. Or the counselor may also refer the student to places where they could get other kinds of help.

The middle school years can feel a lot like the now-closed Disneyland attraction Mr. Toad's Wild Ride. There are lots of zigs and zags. You often feel like you are just moments away from total destruction. When the going gets roughest and you and your middle schooler seem to be bumping heads over everything from hair color to homework, remember my sister's two top phrases for parenting a child through the middle years: "Oh, well." "Not today."

6

QUESTIONS PARENTS SHOULD ASK ABOUT HIGH SCHOOL

It's a little childish and stupid. But then, so is high school.

—Ferris Bueller, *Ferris Bueller's Day Off*

Adolescence is an inside job.

—Madeline Levine, *Ready or Not*

You lived through the 2:00 a.m. feedings. Your adolescent has acquired basic social skills like chewing with their mouth closed (at least most of the time). So why does high school have you so panicky?

It's a time of real change—but, of course, that's true of elementary school and middle school as well. Perhaps the agita comes because you feel like this is the *last* big change in your teen's life that you're going to be able to influence in any real way.

Also, in many cases, there are driver's licenses involved. If there is anything that strikes more terror into the heart of a parent than seeing their child drive away in a car . . . it's seeing their child drive away in a car driven by another teen.

Parents really should not enter the high school parenting land mine without a much better understanding of how teens' brains develop. The American Academy of Child and Adolescent Psychiatry has pointed out that different parts of the teenage brain develop at different ages. In particular, the prefrontal cortex, which governs things like advance planning, does not really develop until about age 25. (Clearly, those rental car companies that didn't allow anyone under the age of 25 to rent their cars knew something!) That means that adolescents are more likely to act on impulse, get into accidents, and engage in dangerous behavior. They are *less* likely to think before they act or think through the consequences of their actions.[1]

105

That, of course, is why they have you. Since teens are not good at thinking things through, you help them do that. You talk through potential sticky situations before they go to the party. You help them backward-plan so they don't end up having to choose between writing their research paper and going to the junior prom.

While parents are doing that, they also need to help their teen with the enormous job of developing an independent identity. From learning basic life skills to developing confidence in their ability to solve problems, high school students need to be given a chance to do things for themselves. So if you've been a helicopter parent (see Question 5 in Chapter 1), perhaps it's time to land the aircraft or give your teen a chance to take over.

This does not mean that you will always agree with their choices, of course. They will wear clothing you probably hate. They may do things to their hair that make you want to weep. So even more than when you were living through the middle school years, pick your battles. Black nail polish? Can't you live with that except possibly when Grandma comes to visit? A pierced nose? Again, you decide. (And in the interest of full disclosure, this was my personal line in the sand—no holes, no tattoos.)

But alcohol? Drugs? Feel free to carve out a very firm no.

Here are some key questions parents should ask as they navigate the high school years.

43. CAN PLAYING IN THE BAND *REALLY* GET MY KID INTO COLLEGE?

Is it really true that parents who want their kids to go to college should make sure they play in the band? Absolutely. In fact, there are two reasons why playing in the band can be such a help for students. The first is academic. The second has to do with the way schools are organized.

On the academic side, there's plenty of evidence, dating back decades, that students who study music do better in school. "Students who learned to play a musical instrument in elementary and continued playing in high school not only score significantly higher but were about one academic year ahead of their non-music peers with regard to their English, mathematics and science skills," said Peter Gouzouasis, professor of music education at the University of British Columbia, who has studied the effects of music education on academic achievement for more than two decades.[2]

It makes sense when you think about it. Music students learn to read music notation (which is a lot like learning to read math equations). They improve their listening skills. They develop eye–hand–mind coordination and acquire team skills. Kids in a band learn to work together to achieve a goal. And the old adage "Practice makes perfect"? It was likely a music teacher who first started saying that to a student who was just sitting down to play scales and other exercises. Unsurprisingly, these same skills translate into success in other classes.

But there's another very practical reason why you should want your kid in the band. Otherwise, the advice could be to enroll your child in any music class. Band matters because of the realities of how schools build their class schedules. In short, band drives the rest of the schedule.

Although the process of building a schedule varies a little from school to school, there are some constants. Typically, students are given a list of courses from which they can choose. Then the administrative juggling begins.

If too few students want a class, it might be combined with another similar course (Spanish IV and Spanish V, for example). Otherwise it cannot be offered. And whenever possible, schools do not want to create a schedule that forces students to choose between, say, Latin IV and advanced calculus, so they are unlikely to be scheduled during the same period. On the other hand, Spanish IV students are unlikely also to enroll in French IV, so those two upper-level courses could be scheduled at the same time.

Band is, in most schools, offered only once. It is typically also the largest class in the school. That makes it a particularly complicated class because it generates a large number of conflicts. And it's filled with students who take advanced classes like AP or IB courses.

When the *Pittsburgh Post-Gazette* interviewed school administrators about the challenges of building a schedule, they often mentioned that band, a singleton, is the toughest to schedule, and thus usually scheduled first. Band is also full of students who want to take AP classes. If those AP courses are themselves also singletons, then band students will all end up in AP classes together. And odds are, that means they'll also be together in several other courses.[3] In other words, band gives students a built-in peer group.

The band is filled with exactly the kids you want in your child's class. If you are looking for a peer group filled with kids who will say, "I can't go out tonight. We have a chemistry test tomorrow," then band is where you're likely to find them.

Several years ago, a group of musicians from my church decided to put that theory to the test. We created a mentoring program for first-generation students who were both academically inclined and talented in music. We called it the Kids of Note (KON). Our belief was that if we could keep these kids in the band, we could get them into college.

John Rey Tangaran, who played in the West Potomac High School band and is now a student at Virginia Tech, said he realized the benefits of hanging out with band kids early on. "I knew a lot of band kids from AP, and I knew a lot of AP kids from band," he said. He liked being in the band "because it was full of people who actually wanted to learn. When I was in regular and even honors classes, there were lots of people who just wanted to mess around. They would just bring me down."

Jonathan Amaya confirmed the crucial role that band played in helping him, like John Rey, become the first person in his family to go to college. "In my neighborhood," Jonathan said, "not a lot of people were taking honors or IB [International Baccalaureate] classes." But in high school, the fact that he was in the band meant that his other academic classes were with fellow band members who were also serious students. "I realized from them that if I just studied a little harder, I could end up with an A instead of a B."

Astrid Garcia, a Mount Vernon High School student now at William & Mary, found that being in the band with the best students in the school offered another advantage. "If I was having trouble understanding something in a class, there was usually someone in the band I could ask for help," she said.

And as it turned out, the KON provided its own peer group. Every KON understood the challenge of having to interrupt their own studies so they could serve as the family translator. They knew what it was like to worry about a family crisis in a way that most middle and high school students do not. And they knew that just as the other KON were overcoming challenges, they could as well.

Our KON program confirmed some of our beliefs and surprised us in other ways. Expectations for these kids were, far too often, lower than they should have been. Too often, they were told to settle for the less challenging opportunity. But we supported them and prodded them when they needed it. At this writing, five of the six are on track to earn a college degree and the sixth is in an apprenticeship program, leading to a high-skill, high-wage job.

It was, however, not always easy for these first-generation students to keep band in their schedule. Kristi Thomas, a retired elementary school band director who taught the KON, said that she sat in meetings where middle school counselors discouraged her students from continuing with band in middle and high school. "They'd say things like, 'You really ought to take a keyboarding class or sign up for something like mechanical drawing,'" she said.

That's what happened to Jonathan when his high school counselor presented him with a schedule that made it impossible for him to continue with band in his junior year. "I spent three days figuring out how I could get all my other courses and keep band on my schedule," Jonathan said. "I basically had to act as my own counselor."

Both Jonathan and Astrid believe that the leadership they showed in band—Jonathan as a section leader, Astrid as the captain of the color guard—were helpful as they competed for college admission and college scholarships. "Leadership and commitment, that's what playing in the band demonstrated," Jonathan said.

As a parent, don't be surprised if you get the same message about letting students drop out of band in middle school. Be prepared to push back, especially if you want your kid to spend time with the smartest kids in the school.

Go ahead and buy your kid that trombone or clarinet. Suffer through those first renditions of "Let's Go Band." Sell the oranges (or candy bars, or holiday wreaths). You'll be giving your child a first-class educational experience. And you'll be ensuring that your kid is in classes with the school's top students.

Jonathan, John Rey, and Astrid are certainly proof of the impact band can have. All were admitted to excellent schools. Jonathan was named Centennial Scholar at James Madison University, and Astrid was awarded a Presidential Scholarship at William & Mary. John Rey was admitted to the engineering program at Virginia Tech. As a junior, Jonathan earned a spot on the president's list (all As) in his engineering studies.

His secret to getting good grades in college? He said he learned it in band. "You'll do better if you hang out with the smart kids."

44. MY TEEN IS ABOUT TO ENTER HIGH SCHOOL. IS THAT TOO EARLY TO START THINKING ABOUT WHAT COURSES THEY WILL NEED TO TAKE TO GET INTO A GOOD COLLEGE?

Figuring out what colleges are looking for in a prospective student is pretty much like trying to crack the Enigma code. The kid who seemed like a slam dunk for admission is turned down. Sometimes, you can figure it out—the family of a student who was admitted gave millions to the college. The orchestra needed a first-chair violin. Or (and we all know it), the admitted student had a wicked three-point shot.

Most of those are things you can't control, especially if your teen is interested in a highly selective college, one that accepts fewer than one third of the people who apply. But there is one thing teens can control and that is the high school class schedule they set for themselves.

High school students should prepare as though they were going to the Ivy League. First, this gives students as many options as possible. Coursework that meets Harvard's standards will also be a selling point if your teen applies to UVA or Carleton. If a senior decides not to apply to the Ivy League, but instead to Home Town U, do you think the college will be unhappy that they show up with four years of math? Yeah, me either.

Second, taking a challenging curriculum in high school may even mean that your teen graduates from college early. Many schools grant college credit for high scores on AP or IB tests. So your teen's hard work in high school could save you a year of tuition. Because of AP, IB, and dual enrollment classes, a growing number of students arrive on campus with a semester's worth of course credits already completed.

Third, following these recommendations will not only help your teen get *into* college, it will make sure they can be successful once they get there. Today, far too many high school graduates are not academically ready for college. Surveys by the nonprofit organization Youth Truth have found that fewer than half of all high school students feel prepared to do university-level work.[4] Nearly half —44%—said they wish they'd worked harder in high school, and 47% said they wish they'd taken different (harder) classes.[5]

Kids don't know at the beginning of their high school career where they're going to want to go to college or what they want to study. Heck, Michael Jordan didn't know he was going to grow 4 inches over the summer so he could make the varsity team. But he practiced *as though* he would.

So that's the lesson. Prepare as though the Ivy League is on the horizon. Your teen won't regret it.

But what does that academic preparation look like? The New Trier School District in Illinois, one of the nation's finest public school systems, has a student body filled with kids who are aiming for the most selective colleges in the country. They have suggested that students consider the following minimums when making their course selections:[6]

Table 6.1.   Suggested Course Requirements for College Admissions for Highly Selective Colleges

English	4 years
Mathematics	4 years*
Foreign Language	4 years
Lab Science	3–4 years
Social Studies	3–4 years
Academic Electives (Art, Music)	2 years

Table 6.2.   Suggested Course Requirements for College Admissions for Public Universities

English	4 years
Mathematics	3–4 years*
Science	3 years
Social Studies	3 years
Academic Electives (Art, Foreign Language,* Music)	2 years

Table 6.3.   Suggested Course Requirements for College Admissions for Private 4-Year Colleges

English	4 years
Mathematics	3–4 years
Foreign Language	3 years
Science	3 years
Social Studies	2–3 years
Academic Electives	2 years

(*High school courses taken in Grades 7 and 8 are included. For example, Algebra I, plane geometry, and the first year of any foreign language would be included in this total.)

If you are the parent of a student of color, you need to push especially hard to ensure that your high schooler is enrolled in this challenging course of study. The Education Trust, a national research and advocacy organization focused on educational equity, has noted that Black and Latino students are assigned to advanced courses at much lower rates than their peers.[7] Yet the organization's research has shown that when admitted to these classes, students perform equally well regardless of ethnicity.

Taking these classes is a key step in ensuring that your student will be able to attend the college of their choice. It's a fight worth having.

45. DO ADVANCED PLACEMENT AND INTERNATIONAL BACCALAUREATE CLASSES MATTER?

The short answer here: yes. Advanced Placement (AP) and International Baccalaureate (IB) classes matter. A lot.

These advanced classes offer a number of benefits for students. First, they help teens who are applying to selective colleges or universities. Typically, AP or IB classes are the most rigorous classes offered in any school.

Students who aspire to attend a selective university need to demonstrate their willingness to tackle this challenging curriculum.

Second, they can boost a student's grade point average since many schools offer a GPA bonus for IB/AP classes. Fairfax County, Virginia, students, for example, earn a weighted grade bonus of 0.5 (so an A in an IB class gives students a 4.5 for purposes of computing their grade point average). The theory is that students will be more inclined to take challenging classes if their GPA doesn't suffer. That's why you see colleges requiring a GPA of "4.0 or higher," as Princeton specifies. Students who do not take AP or IB courses, then, place themselves at a competitive disadvantage, since their GPA will be lower than other students at their school who accepted the challenge. With many colleges offering merit scholarships to students with high grades, a high GPA can save you tuition money.

Scores on the AP exam can earn college credit. Some (but not all) colleges will give college credit for students who have taken these classes and met a threshold score on the exam. Given the cost of college tuition, these extra college credits may allow students to graduate a semester or year early (or, given today's crowded campuses, at least finish in the expected four years). These extra credits can also allow students to take additional classes while on campus or to take a reduced schedule for a semester or two so they can do well in an especially challenging class.

But most important, AP and IB classes prepare students for the caliber of work they will be expected to do when they get to college. John Rey Tangaran, who took six AP courses (including both AP Physics 1 and AP Physics C) in high school, said he noticed a big advantage when he started his engineering classes at Virginia Tech. "Many of my classmates were complaining about how hard the work was," he said. "I just told them that we had done that last year in AP."

Although both AP and IB are rigorous, there are some differences between the two programs:

Advanced Placement (AP). The College Board created AP in 1956 as a program for a few elite public and private high schools at which seniors and juniors were given college credit for some high-level courses so they would not be bored by having to cover the same material in college. But average high schools—such as East Los Angeles's Garfield High School, portrayed in the movie *Stand and Deliver*—found that the program helped their students too.

Today, according to the College Board, more students are taking AP classes, in more high schools, and they're doing better. In 2020, the College Board offered 38 AP courses, ranging from AP Two-Dimensional Art and Design to AP Chinese Language and Culture. Most are yearlong courses, but some last only for a semester. Roughly 24% of the class of 2019 took at least one AP class and scored a 3 (passing) or higher.[8]

International Baccalaureate (IB). The International Baccalaureate Programme was established in 1968. (Yes, they spell it "Programme," and, yes, it's a bit precious. So from here on out it's just IB.) From the beginning, IB was envisioned as a truly international curriculum, and IB now has a presence in more than 150 countries. But IB's U.S. footprint is smaller, with just under 1,000 schools offering the program.

IB is a comprehensive curriculum that requires students to demonstrate knowledge and skills in six academic areas:

- Language and literature. Languages range from Asante to Xhosa, Yoruba, and Zulu.
- Language acquisition. IB students are expected to speak, read, and write two languages. Options include a wide range of modern languages as well as Latin and classical Greek.
- Individuals and societies. Students choose from 10 subjects (business management, economics, geography, global politics, history, informational technology in a global society, philosophy, psychology, social and cultural anthropology, and world religions).
- Science. Students must take at least one science class (biology; computer science; chemistry; design technology; physics; or sports, exercise, and health science).
- Mathematics. IB math classes are organized differently from the more traditional U.S. approach of algebra, geometry, and so on. Even first-level math courses include content drawn from algebra, functions, geometry and trigonometry, probability and statistics, and calculus.
- The arts. All students are required to complete at least one class in dance, music, theater, film, or visual arts.

Students seeking the full diploma also complete a course called Theory of Knowledge and write an extended essay. Most schools allow students to take one or more IB classes whether or not they are enrolled in the full diploma program.

Which is better? Both programs are terrific. They give students an opportunity to do in-depth reading and writing that they might not get in their regular classes. Astrid, who completed the full IB Diploma at Mount Vernon High School in Fairfax County, reflected on the value of her coursework after completing her freshman year at William & Mary. "When

I was in high school, I thought the workload from my IB classes was a lot—and it was, compared with friends who were not taking IB. But once I got into college, it was nothing compared to the workload I have now."

The biggest benefit for Astrid was how IB taught her to think and analyze. "You are not just expected to learn it, but to analyze it, discuss it, and take it a step further." Those, she said, are skills she uses every day.

In suburban Virginia, where a lot of diplomats are stationed, we found that IB was often the curriculum of choice for international students. Students could move from Virginia to another country if their family was reassigned without losing a step.

However, not all colleges are as familiar with IB. Students who enroll in these classes may need their counselor to explain the value of this challenging curriculum to a college when they apply.

Although there's a strong case to be made that anyone who wants to enroll in AP or IB classes should be able to do so, not all schools agree. In 2013, The Education Trust looked closely at AP and IB participation rates nationally and by school and found that hundreds of thousands of students of color and students from low-income backgrounds were missing out on these opportunities.[9]

But the research shows that when low-income, Black, and Brown students are given the chance to enroll, they succeed in advanced courses.[10] In particular, when lower-achieving students are given the opportunity to enroll in more college prep classes, the likelihood of completing a postsecondary credential increases.

If you are a parent of a student of color, you may need to press hard to make sure your high schooler is allowed to enroll in AP or IB classes. It is well worth the effort.

46. I'VE HEARD STUDENTS CAN TAKE ACTUAL COLLEGE CLASSES WHILE THEY'RE IN HIGH SCHOOL. HOW DO THEY DO THAT?

There's one final way for students to earn credits that will give them a jump start on college or a career. Dual enrollment (DE) programs have existed for more than 50 years, but it is only recently that students and their families have focused on how they can provide the opportunity to complete college faster.

DE programs are partnerships between local education agencies and institutions of higher education that allow students to enroll in college courses and earn transferable college credits while they are still in high school. The college courses they take are offered either free of charge or at a very low tuition rate.

Typically, DE students attend classes on the campus of the college or university located in or near their high school. Sometimes, students may actually be able to take their college class on their high school campus. In other cases, especially if a high school does not offer a particular course that a student is interested in taking, they can look online.

We know that students who take a dual enrollment class are much more likely to enroll in—and complete—a postsecondary degree or certificate program. One study of more than 200,000 high school students who took at least one DE class found that 84% of them enrolled in a community college after graduation. Of that group, roughly half—46%—earned a degree or certificate within five years. Of the students who enrolled in a four-year college after high school, that completion number was higher, at 74%.[11] Both those completion rates are significantly higher than completion rates of students who enter college with no college-level classes.

The state of Georgia offers one example of a highly successful DE program. In operation since 1992, Georgia's DE program allows any student (in public or private school or a homeschooler) to take postsecondary courses at no charge. Students can take degree-level courses such as calculus or an introductory English class. They may also enroll in career courses that will allow them to be trained for specialized careers from health care to building trades. The program pays for tuition and books for every student, with the only student financial responsibilities being course-related fees and transportation. Some Georgia students earn an associate degree or a career-level certificate even before they have their high school diploma.

Not every state offers DE (although it's becoming more popular every year), and the details will not be the same. Some states may limit the number of DE classes a student can take while in high school. Others limit DE to high school juniors and seniors. Your school's guidance counselor is a good source of information on how to take advantage of this opportunity.

All DE course are not equal. Focus on the courses that either meet core requirements (in English, math, social studies, science, or foreign language) or that can help student prepare for a career. Be sure the DE credits will transfer. In 29 states, there are policies requiring public colleges and universities to accept dual enrollment credit with no added restrictions. If your teen will just have to repeat the math or history course next year, it's probably not worth it.

As with other advanced opportunities, however, access to DE programs is sadly not always equitable. So you may need to be a little pushy to make sure your teen gets the opportunity to earn college credit in high school.

47. MY TEEN IS REALLY STRUGGLING IN CLASSES. WHAT'S THE BEST WAY TO HELP?

In elementary and middle school, kids could often get by without studying or working too hard. That generally ends on the first day of high school. Teachers expect more and do much less hand-holding.

If teens are taking challenging courses (and they should), there will probably be homework every night. It will be really tough to watch them struggle, and, especially at the beginning of the school year, they're likely to struggle a fair bit.

The best advice: Support your teen but don't fix the problem. Listen while they talk about—and, OK, probably whine about—how hard they're working. But wherever possible, let them figure out the solution to the problem by themselves.

If your teen is having a tough time with a math class, encourage them to talk to the math teacher. If you do that instead, you'll send the message that they can't handle it by themselves. You could help them develop a list of questions to ask the teacher, but let them take charge.

In fact, encouraging your teen to build a relationship with their teachers is one of the best ways to help them be successful. This is particularly important if your teen would be the first in your family to attend college. One of the keys to success in college is the ability to ask professors for help, so learning how to do that in high school can give your teen a real head start.

When your teen does talk with the teacher, they should ask about any resources the school might provide. The National Honor Society often sets up tutoring sessions to help students in a particular class. There are many online resources, but not all of them are equally good. Have your teen ask the teacher for any recommendations. Teachers sometimes use their lunch period or their planning period to help students catch up. If your teen's teacher does this, they should definitely plan to take part.

48. DOES MY TEEN NEED A TUTOR?

Even after taking the steps outlined in the last question, there may come a time when your teen is still struggling in a particular class. You know one thing for sure: You can't help. They're struggling in Spanish, and you studied German. They're facing daily challenges trying to work math programs in subjects you have long forgotten. Or they are having trouble with chemistry and, well, so did you.

So what do you do? Even if you're willing to try to pitch in to help your teen master tough content, the odds are that you're not the best person to do that. And in the process, you could put a strain on your relationship.

Instead, think about finding a tutor. Research shows that tutoring can be effective in helping high school students improve their academic skills, stay in school, and graduate from high school.[12]

First, have your teen check with the teacher. This will give your teen a good perspective on whether tutoring is the best course of action. It may be that instead they should move from an honors class to a regular class.

Teachers also know if the school provides any free tutoring. In addition to recruiting honor students to tutor, college alumni associations also may provide tutoring. In Fairfax County, for example, MIT alums tutor students in math and science.

Private tutoring can be an expensive proposition, but I've seen cases where it made the difference between passing a class and having to retake it in summer school. Still, no tutoring program will work unless you and your teen have a clear understanding about what you are signing on to:

- Don't wait. Teens typically don't want to admit they need help, even when they do. If your school has a system that allows parents to check on their student's grades, be sure to use it. If by the middle of the first marking period your teen seems to be struggling, you need to start thinking about the best way to address the problem.
- Try to identify the source of the problem. Is your teen doing their homework but not understanding it? Are they so involved with sports and activities that they aren't putting in the time on school-work? Your teen may need a schedule change more than a tutor.
- Schedule enough time. At a first meeting, the tutor should develop a plan to help your teen catch up. If they are a year and a half behind in a foreign language, they won't catch up in four weekly tutoring sessions.

- Tutoring will only work if your teen takes it seriously. Treat it like a class and expect that your teen will do what the tutor asks.
- If you are hiring a private tutor, don't expect them to come to your house. For safety reasons, tutors usually prefer to meet in a public place, such as a public library. Online tutoring may be an option.
- Check in regularly. Be sure your teen feels they are benefiting from the tutoring. And if they do not find it enjoyable, check to make sure they at least think it's effective.

49. HOW CAN A COUNSELOR HELP MY HIGH SCHOOLER APPLY TO COLLEGES?

If your teen is enrolled in a small private school, they'll probably spend a lot of time during their senior year with their guidance counselor. If they're in a large public school, they may go a long time without ever checking in.

But Eleanor Saslaw, a retired guidance counselor and guidance director in several Fairfax County middle and high schools, thinks high school students and their families need the help that a counselor can provide. They should start building a relationship in "early 10th grade. That's the best time to help parents and students think about a college choice that would really be best for that individual."

Although Saslaw met with many parents who "just came in with their idea of a brand name college or two," she was often able to help them think more about other colleges that might be a better fit. "The counselor can help parents not to have an automatic prescription of what their high schooler should do or needs to do. Counselors can help parents develop an appreciation for their child's personal strengths and weaknesses."

Counselors may also know about a program at a college that could be a game changer. That's what happened to Camilo Rodriguez during his senior year at Mount Vernon High School in Fairfax County. Camilo was accepted by the University of Mary Washington (UMW), about an hour's drive from home. But he didn't know a lot about the school, and very few students from his high school went there.

Then his high school counselor told him about the Student Transition Program (STP), a summer on-campus program that would help him with the transition from high school to college. "It was an optional program but if I chose to do it, it would be completely paid for," he said. "At first, I wondered why I'd want to start college early." Then he realized that STP could give him a jump start on earning credits, and he could earn them for free. He went to UMW, enrolled in STP, and completed the summer with, among other things, a statistics course already accomplished.

For many selective colleges, a counselor letter is an important part of the application package. Since counselors see many students in a large high school, my advice is to help the counselor write that letter. Have your teen assemble a bulleted listing of the key things they would like the counselor to emphasize. When we did this, my daughter just said, "I know you're really busy so here's something to help you write my letter."

Your teen may not be thinking about a four-year college. Counselors can help them sort through other options: community college, a job training program or apprenticeship, or enlisting in the armed forces. All these can be good choices for individual students, but it's best to make them with a trusted and unbiased adviser.

Yes, counselors still are helpful throughout high school for all the reasons discussed in Question 42 in Chapter 5. But every student needs to see the counselor during senior year.

50. MY YOUNG ATHLETE HOPES TO PLAY NCAA (NATIONAL COLLEGIATE ATHLETIC ASSOCIATION) DIVISION I ATHLETICS. WHAT SHOULD WE BE DOING TO MAKE SURE THEY ARE ELIGIBLE?

The NCAA enforces rules for potential Division I athletes. During their four years in high school, athletes are expected to accumulate 16 "core course" credits. Only classes in English, math (Algebra I or higher), natural or physical science, social science, foreign language, comparative religion, or philosophy may be approved as NCAA core courses. Remedial classes and classes completed through credit-by-exam are not considered NCAA core courses.

As a practical matter, athletes hoping to play Division I athletics should check carefully with their coach and the guidance department. Each year, they should successfully complete at least four solid academic courses—in English, math, science, social studies, and foreign language.

If there is one aspect of parenting that brings out even worse behavior than the college application process, it is youth athletics. Parents get seduced by the possibility that their little Johnny or Jessica will earn a Division I scholarship and then go on to play as a professional athlete. And some do.

Just not very many. According to the NCAA, of the 1,006,013 high school football players, roughly 2.9% can expect to play Division I football.[13] Of the 399,067 women playing basketball in high school, just 1.3% will play in Division I. A tiny fraction of those athletes may earn a professional contract.

Yet if you go to any youth athletic event, you're sure to find the parents who style themselves as another LaVar Ball. They yell. They coach their own child and seem to take particular delight in berating their young athlete for every misstep. It's no wonder that many young athletes say that the worst part of the game is the ride home in the car.

It's unpleasant for every athlete on the team. It's particularly awful for their own son or daughter. And the reality is that only in an infinitesimal number of cases will all that sideline parental involvement even work. A growing number of youth athletic leagues make parents sign behavior contracts before their kids are allowed to play.

Playing sports teaches kids lots of important lessons. Students who can play in both high school and college will have an experience that will shape them forever. But here's a case where your job as a parent needs to be to step back and let the coach be the coach.

51. MY DAUGHTER WANTS TO GO TO A PARTY WHERE I AM AFRAID THERE WILL BE ALCOHOL (AND MAYBE DRUGS). SHE SAYS THAT IF SHE STAYS HOME, SHE'LL LOSE ALL HER FRIENDS. WHAT DO I DO?

As previous questions have discussed, peer pressure is a fact of life throughout your child's school year. But in high school, the consequences seem to get higher. Instead of begging you for a ridiculously expensive pair of shoes, they want to ride in a car with older kids you may not know. Instead of wanting to watch a movie that's racier than you prefer, they suddenly want to go to parties where that racy behavior may be going on in real life.

The key is to prepare your teen for a sticky situation *before* it occurs. Before they go out, talk about what they might do if they find themselves in a bind. And if there's a proposed party or activity that you think is very likely to be risky (e.g., because parents are not at home), reserve your right to say no.

Also teach your teen how to say no. There are times when the shortest response is the easiest. So have your teen role-play a situation in which they say, "No, thanks." They could say, "I've got a test the next day, so I can't go." Or they could try, "The coach really doesn't want us going out before a game." And of course there's always the easiest and most truthful: "My mom would kill me."

Develop a backup plan. There may come a time when even the most careful teen ends up in a situation that makes them feel uncomfortable. That's when a family code word can come in handy. Agree on a phrase that means, "Come and get me right away." Blogger Bert Fulks has called this the *X-plan*. Your teen texts you the letter X. In return, you send a text that says, "Something's come up. I have to come get you right away. Be ready in five minutes." That allows your teen to save face but also gets them out of a risky situation.[14]

Help your teen find friends who also want to avoid these sticky situations. It is possible to turn peer pressure into positive pressure. And really, there are plenty of high school students who do not drink or use drugs—your teen just needs to find them.

52. I'VE JUST DISCOVERED MY TEEN IS SENDING AND RECEIVING SEXUALLY EXPLICIT PHOTOS. WHAT DO I DO?

You looked at a text message on your teen's cell phone and . . . yikes. The photos were definitely X-rated. This practice, which the National Center for Missing and Exploited Children has defined as "youth writing sexually explicit messages, taking sexually explicit photos of themselves or others in their peer group, and transmitting those photos and/or messages to their peers" by smartphone, computer, video camera, digital camera, or video game, is known as *sexting*.[15]

If you're worried, you're not alone. More than half—57%—of parents of teens say they worry about their teen receiving or sending explicit images, including about one quarter who say this worries them a lot, according to a Pew Research Center survey of parents.[16] And the Pew Center also found that 25% of teens have received explicit images they didn't ask for, and 7% said they knew that explicit images of them had been shared without their consent.[17]

Teenage girls are more likely than boys to say they've received explicit images they did not ask for. That's especially true for older teen girls as 35% of girls ages 15 to 17 have received unwanted explicit images.[18]

State laws—and yes, sexting is illegal in many states—do not have a consistent definition of what "sexually explicit" means. A 2019 article in the journal *Pediatrics* noted that in roughly half of all states, teens who engage in sexting "can be prosecuted, convicted, and sentenced to up to 20 years in prison and receive a lifetime sexual offender status for production and possession of child pornography."[19]

So you're right to be concerned. Despite their claim that "everyone" is sexting, a meta-analysis (analysis of many different studies) finds that somewhere between one quarter and one third of teens engage in the behavior.[20] Still, the numbers don't really matter when it's *your* kid. Here is the talk you need to have with your teen. And you need to have it now.

- Teens who have grown up on social media tend to forget that nothing is ever truly private. The "www" in those email URLs, after all, stands for "World Wide Web." And worldwide is where that picture could end up—your teen sends it to a close friend, but they forward it. And soon, yes, even if it's on Snapchat, it's everywhere.
- Help them think about the future. They may take the picture off their phone, but how about everyone else who received it? How will your teen feel if a college admissions officer sees the picture? How about a potential employer?
- Was it their idea to send the photo in the first place? If a boyfriend or girlfriend has pushed them into sexting, then you have a bigger problem on your hands than a single explicit photograph. In that case, you need to talk about the importance of being with a partner who understands and respects boundaries.
- Do you know who is sending and receiving messages from your teen? You'd know their friends if they came into your home. You should expect no less from online friends, especially since teens sometimes consider someone they have only met online (and not IRL—in real life) as a friend. Be sure your teen knows that they need to set limits on what they share with these friends.
- Check out your teen's online profile. Go on Snapchat, Instagram, and the other social networks where your teen may be communicating with friends. Remind them that they've already chosen to make this information public. You are not snooping. You're just checking out what everyone else already knows.

53. MY TEEN WANTS AN AFTER-SCHOOL JOB. SHOULD I SAY YES?

For many years, nearly everyone—educators, parents, policy makers—praised the value of after-school jobs. They helped students become more responsible. They helped them learn how to manage their time. Although experts still believe that jobs can help teens learn to manage their time and earn money, educators and psychologists are concluding that, in many cases, teen jobs do more to foster bad grades than to advance the work ethic.

Data from the Bureau of Labor Statistics found that the number of teens in the workforce is declining. That trend is expected to continue.[21]

While teens may be learning some skills through their part-time work (such as the importance of showing up on time), the reality is that most teens work in the fast-food industry or in other retail stores. Typically, employers expect teenage employees to be available for irregular hours and on short notice. Neither of these is conducive to good study habits.

The key seems to be not whether students work, but how much time they spend on the job. The *Harvard Education Letter* cites several research studies showing that teens who work more than 15 hours a week

- get poorer grades;
- take less challenging classes;
- are less engaged with school;
- are more likely to use drugs and alcohol (students who work more than 20 hours a week are 33% more likely to use drugs and alcohol);
- are more likely to suffer from depression or anxiety; and
- are less likely to go to college.[22]

Teens often get jobs to help defray college costs. However, you should be aware that your teen's earnings may limit their total financial aid award. For dependent students (those whose parents will be paying at least part of the costs) the FAFSA (Free Application for Federal Student Aid) doesn't count earnings that total $6,600 or below.

Creative teens can sometimes find other ways to earn money. That's what Eric Soller did when he turned 16. He had expected that his parents were going to buy him a car for his birthday. So when they blindfolded him and walked him out to the driveway, he was pretty excited. "But when I opened my eyes, there in the driveway was a brand-spanking-new cardboard box that read 'EZ push lawn mower.'"

Their thought was that he'd relish the chance to work and save up money for a car. Which eventually he did try. But most of his neighbors already had someone to mow their lawns or were content doing that chore themselves. Then Eric found a different paying job when he auditioned for, and was cast in, a dinner theater production of *The Sound of Music*. Actually, "paying job" was almost a misnomer, as he had small roles in small productions in small theaters. "I was paid about the same each night acting at the dinner theater as I would have been for mowing a lawn." As an added benefit, he could use his offstage time to study his AP Biology. So for the rest of his high school career, his part-time job was acting in dinner and community theater.

Some kids sell knives door to door. (In a political campaign, if you were hiring someone for fieldwork, you snatched up anyone who had sold knives because they were utterly fearless about knocking on doors.) Some tutor younger kids for pay. Some consult with tech-impaired neighbors who are likely to be repeat customers. In other words, teens don't have to think about a job only as an opportunity to ask people if they'd like fries with their order.

54. NO ONE IN OUR FAMILY HAS EVER GONE TO COLLEGE. BUT WE THINK MY TEEN COULD BE THE FIRST. WHAT ARE SOME THINGS OUR FAMILY SHOULD KNOW?

A college education is supposed to be a great leveler. And for years, we have told students that earning a degree can be a ticket out of poverty.

That's still true. But for students who come from families that lack "college knowledge," it has gotten more and more difficult to achieve that goal. Nationwide, potential first-generation students are less likely to apply to, attend, or graduate from college.

Question 43 discussed the program Kids of Note (KON), designed to help first-generation students get into college. Here are some of the lessons learned:

- It is critical that your teen take the challenging curriculum outlined in Question 44. You don't want them to find out in October of their senior year that a college they would really like to attend requires four years of science and they have only three.
- Do not be surprised if your teen is not given the advice to take the most challenging courses. At least one of our KON was originally scheduled into a less challenging math class than the one on the recommended list. When he talked with the counselor, he was advised that perhaps he shouldn't try such a tough class in his freshman year. He insisted. He is, as of this writing, a senior engineering major who earned a 4.0 last year.

- Don't automatically assume that you can't afford college. Many universities have programs for first-generation students that will allow them to graduate with little or no debt. In fact, attending one of these colleges may turn out to be much less expensive than going to Home Town U. For example, Dartmouth meets 100% of a family's financial needs once the parents' contribution is determined through the FAFSA and the school's college scholarship program. At Brown, a family earning less than $60,000 with assets less than $100,000 pays nothing.
- Community college is often a low-cost way to start. However, check for grants in your state to see whether a four-year college might actually net out to cost less. The Institute for College Access and Success (TICAS) has found that in California, low-income students may pay less to attend a four-year state institution than they do at a community college. The reason? State assistance for the four-year college more than wipes out the difference in cost.[23]
- Look for colleges that have special programs for first-generation students. Just as our KON supported each other in high school, your first-generation student will need support in college.

Organizations set up to help first-generation students get accepted into college

A Better Chance (ABC) (www.abetterchance.org)
This national organization, founded in 1963, recruits, places, and supports students enrolled in Grades 4 through 9 at more than 300 independent day, boarding, and select public schools. The mission of the organization: "Our mission is to increase substantially the number of well-educated young people of color who are capable of assuming positions of responsibility and leadership in American society."

Students in Grades 4–9 can apply for scholarships to attend independent schools if they meet these criteria:

- identify as a person of color—Black/African American, Asian American/Pacific Islander, Latino/Hispanic, Native American, or multiracial (and they identify with one of the prior ethnicities mentioned);

- consistently perform at or above grade level in math and English;
- have an overall academic average of a B+ or better;
- rank in the top 10% of their class;
- participate in extracurricular activities, both within and outside of the school community;
- demonstrate leadership potential in school or through activities outside of school;
- receive good teacher recommendations; and
- are of upstanding character.

ABC does not provide scholarships. However, ABC does work with families to help them qualify for financial aid.

Advancement Via Individual Determination (AVID) (www.avid.org)
AVID partners with middle and high schools to train teachers so they can in turn prepare all students for success in college, career, and life. Each year, nearly 85,000 educators learn skills and techniques that help them to close the opportunity gap. AVID provides the support that educators and students need to encourage college readiness and success. Research shows that AVID students have outperformed national averages in key college and career success measures. First-generation low-income AVID alumni who go to college are 4 times more likely to graduate than their national peers.

College Possible (www.collegepossible.org/)
College Possible is designed to serve low-income high school students who do not otherwise have the resources or the guidance to earn admission to a four-year college or university. The organization provides a two-year, after-school curriculum to high school juniors and seniors including SAT and ACT test preparation services, college admissions and financial aid consulting, and guidance in the transition to college.

Staffed by volunteers (currently AmeriCorps volunteers), College Possible counselors supplement the work of high school guidance counselors who often do not have the time to provide the one-on-one support that first-generation students need to move through the college application process.

College Possible's Summer Bridge program stays in touch with high school seniors after they graduate to ensure that they *enroll* in the college or university that has accepted them. Each year, up to 40% of the low-income students who are accepted into college do not show up on campus. Financial issues, paperwork, and a worry about fitting in are all reasons students do not enroll in college. Summer Bridge counselors work with students to ensure that they do.

There is no cost for students to participate in College Possible. There is also currently no cost to partner high schools.

iMentor (www.iMentor.org)

iMentor pairs high school students with a college-educated mentor who commits to helping guide them through the college application process for at least three years. The organization, based in New York City but also operating currently in Baltimore, the Bay Area, and Chicago, works in low-income communities where a majority of students served will be first-generation college students. In those schools, each student has a mentor. Mentors help prospective college students apply for scholarships and give advice and feedback on the college application process.

The Posse Foundation (www.possefoundation.org)

The Posse Foundation helps students who might be missed by traditional admissions criteria gain admission to selective colleges and be successful when they enroll. Scholars attending a particular school are placed in groups of 10—a Posse. They provide support for each other, and the foundation supports them with mentoring. Posse Scholars, who all receive full-tuition scholarships from partner colleges, graduate at a rate of 90%.

7

QUESTIONS PARENTS SHOULD
ASK ABOUT NEXT STEPS
AFTER HIGH SCHOOL

If you're a parent who's pushing your kids relentlessly and narrowly
toward one of the most prized schools in the country and you think
that you're doing them a favor, you're not. You're in all probability
setting them up for heartbreak, and you're imparting a questionable
set of values.

—Frank Bruni, *Where You Go Is Not Who You'll Be*

The original plan for this book ended with the happy scene of a high
school senior walking across the stage wearing a cap and gown and
clutching a diploma. But that would not do today's readers any favors. The
last, and in some ways the most important, task of a high school senior is
to prepare for whatever level of schooling comes next.

This was not always the case. For most of the 20th century, students
knew that they could walk straight from the graduation stage into a pretty
good job. Factories hired people with high school educations and those jobs
enabled people to live a middle-class life.

But today's economy requires a higher level of education than ever
before. Nearly all the good-paying jobs require at least some education
after high school. In fact, 80% of the jobs that pay at least $35,000 per
year require post–high school education. More than half (56%) require a
bachelor's degree.[1] That means that no student should graduate from high
school without a clear plan of how they will get the skills they need to be
successful.

That does not mean that every student needs to attend a four-year
college. It particularly does not mean that students need to engage in the
frenzy that seems to have taken over the college application process. In too

many cases, people have apparently lost their minds about getting a high school senior into college.

Wealthy parents (including those described in Chapter 1, Question 5) spend tens of thousands of dollars on tutors and test prep and college counselors. Meanwhile, kids who would be the first in their family to go to college can't afford the test prep and the hand-holding. And their high school counselors, usually busy beyond belief, rarely have time to do much more than remind them of the dates of the SATs and ACTs. The result is a system that doesn't work well for anyone.

This chapter is not an in-depth and detailed look at every step of the college admissions process. Here are a few superb books that tackle that process with great insight and depth: Jeffrey Selingo's *Who Gets In and Why* is certainly the place to start. You should also read Frank Bruni's *Where You Go Is Not Who You'll Be*, Julie Lythcott-Haims's *How to Raise an Adult*, and Joie Jager-Hyman's *B+ Grades, A+ College Application*.

This chapter focuses on a few places where parents seem to ask the most questions or that seem to be the biggest pain points. First, how does your family figure out where your teen should apply? Even in the era of the Common App, kids have to have some realistic notions about where they want to go and where they can actually get in.

Second, how can parents survive the application and essay-writing process without actually writing the essay themselves? (And here's a tip: If you write it, the college admissions officer will know.)

But let's assume your teen has taken that challenging curriculum. They have worked hard and have earned a decent GPA. What comes next? Where should they think about applying? Here are the questions parents should ask.

55. IS IT BETTER FOR MY
TEEN TO TAKE THE ACT OR THE SAT?

Until recently, this wasn't even a question. Colleges chose which test, ACT or SAT, they would accept. In general, if you wanted to go to college on the East or West Coast, you took the SAT. If you were going to college in the Midwest, you took the ACT. (That was one reason why Iowa students always seemed to do so well on the SAT—only students who were planning to go to college out of state—generally the strongest students—even took the exam.)

But today, more colleges are accepting both the ACT and the SAT—and more students are taking advantage of that option. Since 2018, the numbers of students taking the SAT and the ACT have been relatively equal.[2]

In fact, a growing number of students take both tests and compare their scores. Are you wondering which test is easier? Neither. Both tests are designed to be challenging, and they are.

Still, they are sufficiently different that students may do better on one than the other. The best advice is to take a timed, full-length practice test for each and see which exam seems like it's a better fit.

Here are some things to consider as your teen makes the choice between the ACT and the SAT:

- Have your teen take the PSAT and the PLAN in either their sophomore or junior year. Check with your school counselor—many schools now administer both tests. The scores should give you an idea of whether one test format makes a significant difference.
- If your teen attends a school that gives only one of the two tests, go online to take a practice exam, or take a practice exam through one of the college prep courses. It's important that the practice exam be taken under conditions that are as close as possible to an actual SAT or ACT test.
- Check with the college. A growing number of colleges will accept either the ACT or the SAT. Some will accept only one. If that college is your teen's number one choice, well, then the decision is pretty much made for you.
- The ACT has a section dedicated to science, while the SAT does not. (The SAT reading section does include science content.) If your teen is particularly strong in science, that might argue for switching to the ACT. On the other hand, if your teen does poorly on the ACT science section, consider either making a significant shift in how to study for the test the next time or switching to the SAT.
- Decide if applying only to "test-optional" universities, and forgoing the ACT or SAT altogether, will help your teen.

56. ARE THERE COLLEGES THAT DO NOT REQUIRE EITHER THE SAT OR THE ACT?

Across the country, there are a growing number of colleges that do not require the SAT. Most community colleges admit students whether they

Table 7.1. SAT and ACT Comparisons

SAT		ACT
Reading: One 65-min section 5 passages from literature, history, studies, natural sciences Writing & Language: One 35-min section Grammar, vocabulary, editing skills Math: One 25-min section (no calculator); One 55-min section (w/ calculator)	Test format	English: One 45-min section 5 essays Questions focus on the elements of effective writing Math: One 60-min section Reading: One 35-min section tests reading comprehension Science: One 35-min section Measures the interpretation, analysis, evaluation, reasoning, and problem-solving skills required in the natural sciences Writing: One 40-min essay (optional)
Math and Evidence-Based Reading & Writing scored on a scale of 200–800. Composite SAT score is the sum of the 2 section scores and ranges from 400 to 1600.	Scoring	English, Math, Reading, & Science scores range from 1 to 36. Composite ACT score is the average of your scores on the 4 sections and ranges from 1 to 36.
No	Is there a penalty for wrong answers?	No
3 hrs	Total time	2 hrs 55 mins without writing 3 hrs 35 mins with writing
No—but students may choose not to send the score of a particular SAT test to a college. (However, some colleges require that students submit all scores from every time they took the test.)	Can I combine scores from different tests?	Yes—students can combine scores from several ACT tests. (However, some colleges require that students submit all scores from every time they took the test.)
5 reading passages	Reading	4 reading passages
Arithmetic Algebra I and Algebra II Geometry, trigonometry, data analysis	Math	Arithmetic Algebra I and Algebra II Geometry, trigonometry, probability, & statistics
No science section	Science	1 science section—tests critical thinking rather than specific science knowledge

have taken the SAT or not. These and other "open admission" universities will accept all applicants who have a high school diploma or a GED.

Many other universities do not require a test score for admission, but they take a range of approaches to how they communicate this to students. A *test-optional college* lets students make the decision about whether to submit test scores. Most of these universities will consider SAT or ACT scores if students submit them. However, they focus the admissions process on factors they think are better at predicting a student's success in college—things like high school grades, coursework, and essay.

Test-flexible colleges accept other test scores in place of the SAT or the ACT. These might include an International Baccalaureate exam or an Advanced Placement test. A student applying to an arts program might be asked to submit a portfolio or to audition in lieu of submitting a test score.

Finally, *test-blind colleges* will not consider test scores, even if you submit them. Very few colleges—only about 1%—fall into this category. If you want the most up-to-date listing of test-optional colleges, check the database maintained by the National Center for Fair and Open Testing (www.fairtest.org).

During COVID, many more schools dropped the requirement that students submit a standardized test score, at least for a year. Both the University of California and the Cal State system took a one-year hiatus from requiring test scores. Texas offered admission to either the University of Texas or Texas A&M to students in the top 10% of their high school class. Some colleges waived test scores only for GPAs above a certain level. Minnesota State University, Mankato, for example, noted that it would allow applicants with 3.0 GPAs and who were in the top half of their high school class to forgo submitting test scores.

It will take a year or two before we see whether colleges that went "test optional" during COVID go back to considering test scores. I am skeptical that we have seen the last of the standardized test.

57. IS SKIPPING THE COLLEGE ADMISSION TEST ALTOGETHER A GOOD IDEA FOR MY TEEN?

It depends. For a teen who is just a terrible test taker—and there are some—eliminating test scores from their application could be a good idea. However, that means that every other aspect of your teen's application is likely to be scrutinized even more closely. As a general rule, colleges like more data rather than less.

Note that even test-optional schools seem to discourage students from avoiding the SAT or ACT altogether. The University of Chicago, which made national headlines by eliminating the SAT/ACT requirement, said, "We encourage students to take standardized tests like the SAT and ACT, and to share your scores with us if you think that they are reflective of your ability and potential. Given that many of our peers do require testing, we anticipate that the vast majority of students will continue to take tests and may still submit their test scores to UChicago."[3]

One admissions officer told the *Chicago Tribune* that while students would not be disadvantaged if they didn't submit a test, they probably could be helped if they submitted a good test score. Andy Borst, director of admissions at the University of Illinois, gave an explanation that was, well, equivocal. "We know that some students have taken the test and are very proud of their test scores, and we didn't want to say to a student who got a 1500 (on the SAT), 'Your accomplishment doesn't mean anything,'" he said.[4]

Some schools that are test optional offer guidelines that can shed light on the best decision. George Mason University, for example, suggested that students who don't submit test scores should have a high grade point average and have taken a challenging set of courses. GMU also noted that homeschooled students must submit tests.[5]

Colleges do want to be sure that admitted students can do the work. If your teen has taken a number of AP or IB courses and can submit grades and test scores for those, the SAT or ACT score may be less critical. But note that students who are admitted to these highly selective colleges tend to take a lot of advanced classes. For the class of 2023, according to *The Harvard Crimson*, "[s]tudents who reported taking one or more AP tests took an average of 8 exams."[6]

If your student's high school is well known by the selective university, test scores may be less important in the overall admissions decision. Admissions officers make it their business to know certain schools that produce a number of accepted students each year. So if your teen goes to one of those schools, has taken the tough classes, and has the grades to prove it, perhaps you can chance it.

But most admissions officials at selective colleges see a role for standardized test scores. "They're especially useful for evaluating the rural Midwestern kid who's No. 1 in a graduating class of nine at a high school you don't know," said Paul Thiboutot, dean of admissions at Carleton

College, a liberal arts college in Northfield, Minnesota.[7] "It levels the playing field," he said in another interview. "It helps us gauge the ability of students across the country when there is no uniformity in the strength of the curriculum."[8]

SAT and ACT scores have also been used to determine the amount of merit aid that a school might offer a student. And right now, we don't know what colleges might do to replace those scores in their financial aid formula.

So in general, it's probably wisest for seniors to take the test. Or the tests.

58. MY TEEN HAS VERY GOOD GRADES AND IS A VARSITY ATHLETE. SHOULD THEY THINK ABOUT APPLYING TO THE IVY LEAGUE?

Absolutely. But they shouldn't necessarily expect to get in.

Teens who are athletes actually may be in the best place to understand the realities of applying to a highly selective college. A kid who is great in Little League usually understands whether they have a shot at moving to the next level. A good high school athlete should be pretty clear-eyed about whether they can play in college. Usually this means they can work toward a goal of being the best they can be but not be devastated when the New York Yankees do not sign them right out of high school.

But that's not always true for good students. It's just harder for the student who is at the top of their own high school class to evaluate their chances for going to an Ivy.

Yet that's where families all started aiming during the 1990s and 2000s. Too many parents and students convinced themselves that there were only a few good colleges in the United States, and that if a senior were not accepted into one of that small elite group, their future was nearly over. So they poked and prodded and Photoshopped and paid people to take their kids' tests. And some of them ended up in jail.

Really, the entire premise is wrong. There isn't just a tiny sliver of colleges turning out graduates who go on to successful lives and careers.

Just 18% of the U.S. senators in 2020 went to Ivy League colleges, while roughly 60% went to a university in their home state.[9] If you want to head a major corporation, you might be better off going to Texas A&M, whose alumni head four of the Fortune 100.[10] And of the four people who were at the top of the ballot in the 2020 presidential election, only one,

Donald Trump, graduated from an Ivy League school—and he transferred there after spending his first two years at Fordham.

As for the others, Joe Biden graduated from the University of Delaware and Fordham Law School. Mike Pence's undergraduate education was at Hanover College in Indiana and Indiana University Law School. Kamala Harris's undergraduate degree was from Howard, and her law degree was from the University of California's Hastings College of Law.

Nancy Pelosi, first woman Speaker of the House of Representatives, earned her undergraduate degree from Trinity College in Washington, DC. Mitch McConnell, Senate minority leader, graduated from the University of Louisville and the University of Kentucky College of Law.

There are two conclusions to draw from this list: First, many people who have risen to the highest levels of their professions did not attend an Ivy League college. Second, for people who are thinking about a career that will be closely tied to a geographic area (think politics here), attending a university close to home will actually be an advantage.

A high school valedictorian who sets their sights on the Ivy League should just be aware that there are a lot of high schools and a lot of valedictorians. More valedictorians, in fact, than the collective freshman classes of the entire Ivy League plus Stanford and MIT all put together. (There are roughly 24,000 valedictorians, and the Ivies plus Stanford admit roughly 23,000 students in any given year.) So the odds are not in your favor.

That doesn't mean those valedictorians won't get in anywhere. They will. In fact, it doesn't mean that they won't be able to go to a great college. Again, they will. But they may not get into the one institution that they dreamed about.

59. WHAT FACTORS ARE MOST IMPORTANT WHEN TEENS ARE DECIDING WHERE TO APPLY?

Former Fairfax County guidance director Eleanor Saslaw saw firsthand the transformation in how families approached applying for college. "When I first started out in this business, parents used to be a lot more relaxed about the college process. That relaxed attitude is disappearing," she said. "Parents feel it is so much more important for their senior to get into *the* school of their choice. That leads them to put pressure on the applicants, on the counselors, and on the teachers."

So families need to look for a college that is the best fit for their teen. The first step is to figure out whether a school is even a realistic option.

The National Center for Education Statistics has created the College Navigator (http://nces.ed.gov/collegenavigator/), and this free website should be bookmarked on your computer. Under the admissions section of each college, you'll find average SAT and ACT scores for admitted students whose scores were at the 25th percentile (in other words, 25% of entering students received that score or lower) and the 75th percentile (higher than 75% of admitted students). These are the "middle 50%"—and the range of scores gives you a pretty good idea of what a typical student at that college looks like.

Is your valedictorian thinking about Harvard? A quick check of College Navigator reveals that even if they have a SAT math score of 800, they'd be only in the 75th percentile of students admitted to Harvard. (In other words, fully one-quarter of entering freshmen scored a perfect 800 on the SAT math test.) A score of 740—an excellent score by any standards—places them in the bottom one fourth of students admitted. Put another way, with a SAT math score of 700, that valedictorian better also have a play opening on Broadway or be a member of an All-American team to put Harvard in anything but the "reach school" category.

What if the college is test optional and your teen hasn't taken the test? You'll need to look for other indicators. What percentage of students submitted test scores? (If the answer is 90%, your teen needs to know they're in a smaller pool, which is probably not an advantage.) At Bowdoin, which does not use test scores for admissions, decisions are based on the secondary school record, completion of a college preparatory program, and recommendations.

The website admissions data will help them chart a path in other ways. MIT, for example, accepted just 5% of male applicants, but 11% of female applicants in 2019. So if your daughter is good in math and wants to go to school in Boston, she'll have at least a slightly better chance of getting in at MIT than at Harvard, which accepted just 5% of women who applied.

Here are the most recent scores for selective colleges in three groups—the Ivies, other selective private institutions, and the so-called Public Ivies (superb state schools). These scores, combined with the school's admissions percentage, will give your teen a pretty realistic view of their chances.

Ivy Plus

This group (the eight Ivy League schools plus Stanford and MIT) are sometimes called the "Ivy Plus." They are among the most selective in the country, and their "middle 50%" scores show that. Admission percentages at these schools are also among the lowest in the country. In 2019, Princeton admitted just 4% of all applicants.

Does this mean your teen should not apply to the Ivies? No. But anyone who applies to one of these schools needs to have several backup alternatives.

Selective Private Colleges

The odds of being admitted to an Ivy League school are pretty grim. In the late 1980s, for example, Yale admitted roughly 20% of all applicants. In 2020, it accepted roughly 6.54%.

There are, however, a number of other small private institutions that attract students whose achievement equals that of students in the Ivies. However, because these colleges are a little less well known, they may accept slightly more of the highly qualified students who apply. For example, Carleton accepted 30% of all applicants, compared with Brown's 14%, even though the two had virtually identical "middle 50%" scores. On this list, I'm partial to Macalester, my alma mater, but any of these smaller liberal arts colleges will provide a superb education.

Public Ivies

Especially if cost is an issue (is there a family where cost *isn't* an issue?), don't overlook the public institutions that are often called *Public Ivies*. They provide high-quality education at a much lower cost, especially for in-state students. Even better, most accept higher numbers of students, so the odds of getting in increase. Some of these schools also guarantee admission to in-state students whose grades place them at the top of their class. Here are some "middle 50%" scores for some of these Public Ivies.

Even with all this information about possible schools and reach schools, and with the hard work your teen has put in during high school, the odds are just tough that they will get into the exact school they have dreamed about. That college may overlook them so they can admit the child of a big donor or the first violist that the school orchestra needs. Some colleges will want students who are strong in science and math. Some may be looking for students from disadvantaged backgrounds. And OK, all of them seem to be looking for a great three-point shooter.

But if your teen has taken serious and challenging coursework, participated in activities that are important *to them*, and generally thought about

Table 7.2. Ivy League

"Middle 50%" SAT Scores Fall 2019

	SAT Evidence-Based Reading & Writing		SAT Math		ACT Composite		ACT English		ACT Math	
	25%	75%	25%	75%	25%	75%	25%	75%	25%	75%
Brown	700	770	740	800	33	35	34	36	31	35
Columbia	700	770	740	800	33	35	34	36	31	35
Cornell	680	760	720	800	32	35	33	36	30	35
Dartmouth	710	770	730	790	32	35	33	36	30	35
Harvard	710	770	750	800	33	35	34	36	31	36
MIT	730	770	780	800	34	36	35	36	34	36
Princeton	710	770	740	800	33	35	34	36	31	35
Stanford	700	770	740	800	32	35	34	36	30	35
U Penn	700	760	750	800	33	35	34	36	32	35
Yale	720	770	740	800	33	35	35	36	31	35

Table 7.3.   Selective Private Colleges

"Middle 50%" SAT Scores Fall 2019

	SAT Evidence-Based Reading & Writing		SAT Math		ACT Composite		ACT English		ACT Math	
	25%	75%	25%	75%	25%	75%	25%	75%	25%	75%
Amherst	650	740	660	780	30	34	31	35	27	34
Carleton	670	750	690	790	31	34	N/A	N/A	N/A	N/A
Claremont McKenna	670	730	690	780	31	34	32	35	29	34
Davidson	650	730	660	755	30	33	34	36	32	35
Duke	720	770	760	800	33	35	33	36	29	34
Haverford	680	750	700	790	32	34				
Howard	580	650	550	630	22	27	22	28	20	26
Macalester	660	740	660	770	29	33	29	35	27	32
Middlebury	670	750	690	780	32	34	N/A	N/A	N/A	N/A
Morehouse	500	560	520	583	18	22	17	26	17	25
Oberlin	650	730	630	750	29	33	30	35	26	31
Pomona	690	750	700	790	32	35	34	35	29	35
Reed	670	750	655	770	30	34	31	35	27	33
Spelman	560	630	520	600	22	26	21	27	19	25
Swarthmore	680	750	700	790	31	35	33	35	29	34
Wellesley	680	750	680	780	31	34	33	35	28	33
Williams	700	760	710	790	32	35	34	36	30	35

Table 7.4. Public Ivies

"Middle 50%" SAT Scores Fall 2019

	SAT Evidence-Based Reading & Writing		SAT Math		ACT Composite		ACT English		ACT Math	
	25%	75%	25%	75%	25%	75%	25%	75%	25%	75%
Georgia Tech	630	730	670	780	29	34	29	35	29	34
UC Berkeley	650	740	680	790	31	35	29	34	28	35
UCLA	650	740	650	790	29	35	28	35	27	34
Univ. of Illinois–Urbana-Champaign	600	700	610	770	26	32	25	34	25	33
Univ. of Michigan	660	740	680	790	31	34	32	35	29	34
UNC Chapel Hill	659	730	660	770	28	33	28	35	26	32
Univ. of Virginia	620	720	610	760	27	33	25	35	26	33
Univ. of Wisconsin	630	700	670	780	27	32	26	34	26	31
William & Mary	630	700	670	780	27	32	26	34	26	31
Univ. of Wisconsin	660	740	660	770	30	34	31	35	27	33

the kind of college they'd like to attend, they'll get in somewhere that works. As Frank Bruni said in *Where You Go Is Not Who You'll Be*:

> You're going to get into a college that's more than able to provide a superb education. . . . But your chances of getting into *the* school of your dreams are slim. Your control over the outcome is very, very limited, and that outcome says nothing definitive about your talent or potential. To lose sight of that is to buy into, and essentially endorse, a game that's spun widely out of control.[11]

60. WHAT'S THE BEST ROLE FOR PARENTS TO PLAY DURING THE COLLEGE APPLICATION PROCESS?

I used to talk with parents about the need to back off during the college application process by saying, "After all, you're not going to be there next year when they move into the dorm." But then parents started actually *moving* close to the college their teen was attending.

So let me just follow up by saying, "It is a VERY BAD IDEA to move to the town where your teen is going to college. They need to grow up and you need to let them."

And in order to do that, they need to have some control over their college application process.

Trust that kids have some sort of ESP about whether they will fit in on a campus or not. One of Sara's friends made that determination very early in her first (and as it turned out, only) visit to a college on her list.

Elena and her parents drove to campus and parked in the designated parking lot. Between the time she got out of the car and the time she arrived at the front door of the admissions office, she recognized that the school wasn't right for her. She said to her parents, "There's nobody at this college like me. I'd be miserable here. I shouldn't apply."

Her mom, having just driven several hours to get to the campus on time, gave the usual parental "don't judge a book by its cover" speech. But at the end of the visit when they were in the car on the way home, she told Elena, "There's no one like you here. You'd probably be miserable. Don't feel like you have to apply."

And remember that you are picking a college that's right for your senior—and that there are probably several that could fill the bill. "Sometimes parents are so caught up on the prestige of the college that they aren't making the best choice for their child," Saslaw said.

61. I KNOW THE COLLEGE ESSAY IS REALLY IMPORTANT. AND I KNOW I COULD HELP MY TEEN. WHAT'S THE BEST WAY TO DO THAT?

As an English teacher at Thomas Jefferson High School in Fairfax County, often regarded as one of the best high schools in the country, and then later as a tutor who helps teens as they write college essays, Catherine Colglazier has seen the gamut of parental involvement in the essay-writing process. Even otherwise laid-back parents, she said, can turn into, "not just helicopter parents, but bulldozer parents."

Parents want to be sure their teen showcases all those SAT words they learned in the expensive prep course they just finished paying for. They want their teen to stand out in the crowd. So they make one small edit to what their teen has written. Then they make another. And pretty soon, Colglazier said, she's looking at 19 Google Docs changes, all made by a loving father. That's when she has to deliver this tough message: "The college is actually not interested in accepting a 50-year-old man. And that's what this essay now sounds like."

The goal, she said, is to let your teen be authentically your teen. That involves letting the college know who your teen is, how they think, how they see the world, and if they're a good fit for that particular campus.

What does an "authentic" essay look like? Helping Astrid Garcia edit her essay taught the KON advisers a critical lesson. Her first draft included a lot of general comments on the value she placed on giving back to others. Not bad, certainly, but also something any kid in the universe might have written.

Then in the third paragraph, Astrid had written this sentence: "I was born in a tent." Asking her about that sentence led Astrid to tell the story of how she and her family had come to the United States after the earthquake in El Salvador. It was a fascinating tale, uniquely hers. And she turned it into an essay that no one else could have written. We were pretty sure that when college admissions officers were reading essays, she'd be the only one who opened her essay with that sentence. She was accepted at, among others, the University of Virginia and William & Mary, where she eventually enrolled.

So your kid was probably not born in a tent. But there's something that makes them unique and special. And that's what they should write about.

Colglazier's advice to parents is to lay back as much as you possibly can. Let the essay be your teen's unique voice. Because, really, the college will know if it isn't.

As always, the writing advice of "Show, don't tell" applies to the essay, Colglazier said. Once your teen has written a draft, have them do a global search for "I." That's a sure signal that they're telling, not showing.

While you should not write the essay, you should look over the application before it is finally submitted. Kristi Thomas, who did the final read for a number of KON students, said that students sometimes missed a question. She also advised saving a PDF of the final application before you send it. "One college told one of our KON that he had not submitted a section of the application." He had the time-stamped PDF and was able to submit it as evidence that the snafu was on their end.

62. OUR HIGH SCHOOL SENIOR DIDN'T GET ACCEPTED BY ANY OF THE COLLEGES THEY APPLIED TO. WHAT DO WE DO NOW?

It seems to be a law of nature that the college rejections arrive before the college acceptances. But what if your senior receives *only* rejection letters to every single college on their list? At that point, it's a little late to say, "We really need to be realistic about which schools we consider to be safety schools." And it's a little late to harken back to the counselor's warning about thinking of Top Choice U as a reach school.

So what happens if your kid didn't make the correct choices in November? What do you do when all the college admissions envelopes say, "Thanks, but no thanks"?

First, don't panic. OK, don't panic in front of your child. This does not mean that your child is forever consigned to jobs that involve asking, "Do you want fries with that?" There are still colleges that have available spaces. You just have to find them.

Here are three ideas.

Have your teen call any schools that put them on the wait list. Read that sentence carefully—it is your *teen* who must do the phoning. Colleges keep careful records of their "yield" (the number of students offered admission who actually enroll). But inevitably, some students who were offered admission will not choose to attend. That's why colleges have wait lists in the first place.

In the phone call, your teen should share any additional information that might help them move up on the wait list. (Winning a state science competition would be helpful. Being voted Mr. Washington High School might not.) If their second semester grades improved significantly, they should also share those with the admissions office.

This is also the time to see if the university has made any program changes that might affect your teen's admission. That's how Canelle Boughton moved herself off the University of Virginia wait list.

"Of the four colleges I applied to, only Boston University accepted me," she recalled. "But when I went to a freshman weekend, I knew BU wasn't the right school for me."[12]

Fortunately, her high school band director knew that the University of Virginia was trying to improve its marching band. As a former high school drum major, Canelle was able to make the pitch that she provided a skill the university needed. That fall, she happily marched off to Charlottesville.

Second, call a counselor who specializes in college admissions. This is a time for triage. You need someone who knows the ropes, who knows the college admissions officers, and who will give both you and your child a clear-eyed view of what is possible. Some high schools have such a person on staff; some do not. Ask your high school counselor for a recommendation.

Third, check out the National Association of College Admissions Counselors (NACAC) website. Each year, NACAC conducts a survey of colleges that are accepting applications after the May 1 deadline, known as the College Openings Update: Options for Qualified Students. You can use the data on the site to find out the schools that still have space available. The survey is updated and remains online until September 1. Go to https://www.nacacnet.org/collegeopenings and click on the state that interests you. Then check out schools that still have space available in their freshman class.

And finally, again, don't panic. It's becoming increasingly common for students to transfer at the end of their freshman year. So if your graduate starts at a college that turns out not to be a good fit, they can apply again for their sophomore year. Sometimes it turns out to be easier to be accepted as a sophomore than as a freshman.

8

QUESTIONS PARENTS SHOULD ASK ABOUT STUDY SKILLS, HOMEWORK, AND WHAT WE KNOW ABOUT BRAIN SCIENCE

The controversy about whether to give kids homework will go on as long as there are teachers to assign it and students to complain about doing it.

—Roberta Tovey

Over the years, homework has come in and out of favor. In 1901, the state of California voted to ban all homework for students under the age of 15. Obviously, that didn't last. More than a century later, schools, parents, and teachers are still struggling with the same issue. Is homework worth it? And if it is, how much is too much? Even in a time of economic uncertainty, when parent are worried about whether their kids will be successful in a tough new economy and thus advocating for more homework, an equally vocal group worries that we are placing too much of a burden on kids, especially the youngest.

Parents still have many questions. Why do teachers assign homework? How can parents help? What should they do if they feel that their child's homework is too much, too hard, or too reliant on busywork?

As researchers study how our brains work, develop, and learn, they are uncovering new insights about homework and how it can affect children's learning. Parents also need to know more about the latest brain science.

So here are the questions you should ask about homework and study skills.

63. SOME PEOPLE THINK HOMEWORK IS IMPORTANT; OTHERS HATE IT. WHAT SHOULD PARENTS KNOW ABOUT THE PROS AND CONS OF HOMEWORK?

The arguments for homework. We know that the amount of time students spend learning a skill directly affects their ability to master it. Practice really does make perfect. We know that parents need and want a way to keep in touch with what their kids are learning. We know that we want to raise children who develop responsibility and a work ethic. Homework can do all those things.

There have been several studies on the effects of homework on student learning. One of the most comprehensive was published in 2006, reviewing research from 1987 to 2003. The study's authors concluded:

> With only rare exceptions, the relationship between the amount of homework students do and their achievement outcomes was found to be positive and statistically significant. Therefore, we think it would not be imprudent, based on the evidence in hand, to conclude that doing homework causes improved academic achievement.[1]

Homework gives students the opportunity to:

- review and practice the skills, concepts, and information they have learned in class;
- get ready for the next day's class;
- learn how to work independently and develop self-discipline;
- develop initiative and take responsibility for finishing what they start;
- learn more about a subject than the teacher can cover in a class period; and
- relate what they are learning in school to their lives outside of school, helping them connect school learning to the real world.

Finally, research shows that homework affects not only *learning*, but *earning*. Northwestern University professor James Rosenbaum reviewed the impact of doing homework on students' education and job prospects. Here's what he found: "Students doing no homework end up with 1.2 years less education and 19 percent lower earnings than average. Students doing 15 hours or more a week of homework attain almost 1.5 more years of education and attain 16 percent higher earnings than average. This 2.7-

year spread in educational attainment and 35 percent spread in earnings are both extremely large (especially considering that these outcomes are associated with variation in self-reported homework time in high school)."[2]

One reason for the difference in earnings, Rosenbaum said, is that high school homework can increase the chances of earning a college degree. Over half the students who do more than 10 hours of homework a week will get a four-year college degree; only about 16% of those doing less than 3 hours of homework a week will earn a bachelor's degree.

Homework also allows parents to play an active role in their child's education. It makes it possible for parents to see their child's progress. This is, of course, assuming parents actually let their kids *do* the homework (remember the nuclear reactor supposedly constructed by the first grader).

The arguments against homework. On the other hand, there are popular arguments against homework. The 2006 book *The Case Against Homework: How Homework Is Hurting Our Children and What We Can Do About It* is critical of both the quantity and the quality of most homework assigned by teachers today. The authors have argued that too much homework harms children's health and limits the time families can spend together. They have also been critical of the lack of training most teachers receive in designing and assigning homework.[3]

Researchers spoke in depth with students in alternative schools, asking them about their decision to drop out of school. "Students told us about chaotic family lives, cramped living quarters, and parents who worked at night. They also kept mentioning their inability to complete homework as a factor in the decision to leave school," the study's authors said in an article in *Educational Leadership*.[4]

(The book and the follow-up article were published in 2000 and 2001, respectively, long before homework that required computers and access to high-speed internet made the digital divide even more of a homework divide. As Chapter 2 discussed, this problem still needs to be addressed.)

Some of the criticisms of homework are valid. Teachers don't always receive training in how to assign effective homework. Kids without access to technology do find themselves on the wrong side of what Jessica Rosenworcel, a commissioner at the Federal Communications Commission, called the *homework gap*.

But we know that every elementary school child would not be climbing trees or writing their own musicals if they weren't doing homework. As Common Sense Media, probably the best source on children and screen time, noted, "On average, 8- to 12-year-olds in this country use just under five hours' worth of entertainment screen media per day (4:44), and teens use an average of just under seven and a half hours' worth (7:22), not including time spent using screens for school or homework."[5]

It's hard to argue that an hour of homework is more valuable than an hour of free play or reading for pleasure. But it's pretty easy to say that an hour of homework is more valuable than an hour of Instagram or TikTok.

An age-appropriate amount of homework (more on that later), with a mix of activities so it's not all just busywork, can be beneficial for student learning. In 2000, the school board of Piscataway, New Jersey, took up the issue of homework and set limits—30 minutes per night for elementary school students, 2 hours for middle and high schoolers.[6] It's worth noting, however, that by 2019, the board's homework policies largely center around an occasional "No Homework Night."[7]

You do need to know your school's policy about homework and how your child's teacher (or teachers) plan to implement it. There is nothing worse than discovering in mid-October at parent–teacher conferences that the teacher your kid told you "never" assigned homework had in fact been waiting for your child to turn it in.

64. WHAT DOES BRAIN SCIENCE SAY ABOUT HOMEWORK?

Like the research reported above, the brain research on homework is mixed. Homework, when it's "short and focused," is helpful in improving students' academic understanding.[8] There's also some evidence that homework can help elementary students build study habits, learn time management, and help them develop self-discipline. However, there is no evidence that if a little homework is good, a lot is better, particularly at the elementary school level.

For secondary students, the evidence supporting homework is stronger. Homework is most effective when it is an integral part of learning rather than an add-on. Providing students with high-quality and timely feedback is also critical. But just as with elementary school students, there is a point of diminishing returns on homework, with between 1 and 2 hours a day (and a little more for the oldest secondary school students) being the sweet spot.

The Education Endowment Foundation, which has assembled a wealth of research on many education topics, has said that attainment boosts of about five months can be expected from students doing homework regularly. The benefits are greater if the homework includes things like completing projects, less if homework is more focused on routine tasks like memorizing vocabulary words.[9]

If you find that the only homework your child ever does is drill-and-practice, you might challenge your child to add in some other learning activities. Take it from a former school board member, though; a suggestion to the teacher that you know better than she does how to assess what students are learning will not be warmly received.

Brain research also is giving us a much better idea of how students should study. Students are more successful when they

- space out their study sessions over time;
- experience the material in multiple modalities;
- test themselves on the material; and
- work to make meaningful connections between new information and things they already know.[10]

65. HOW MUCH HOMEWORK SHOULD STUDENTS EXPECT IN EACH GRADE?

A good rule of thumb is that children should expect to do roughly 10 minutes of homework for each grade level. That's a general guideline supported by both the National PTA and the National Education Association. So first graders would expect about 10 minutes of homework, while fifth graders should do roughly 50 minutes a day.

At the beginning of the year, ask the teacher how much homework they typically assign. If your child usually spends much more—or much less—time than the teacher has suggested, get in touch with the teacher. It might be that the work is too difficult, or not challenging enough. In either case, the teacher might be able to modify at least some assignments so your child is challenged but neither overwhelmed nor bored.

If you find that homework assignments are so numerous and so lengthy that they really do interfere with the time you spend as a family, talk with the teacher about some adjustments. Many schools are adopting revised homework policies that, for example, prohibit a due date for a big project on the day after a school vacation.

66. WHAT ARE GENERAL RULES
FOR HELPING CHILDREN WITH HOMEWORK?

Research on parent involvement in homework is pretty clear: It helps. Of course, that depends on the *way* parents are involved. When parents are supportive, they can boost learning. But when parents do too much (or do it all), they end up having a negative impact on their child's learning. So here's how to help:

Help your child find time for studying. This means making homework a priority. On most days, there should be a predictable time for homework.

Experiment to find your child's best time for studying. Some people are "night owls" and work best in the evening. Others are "morning birds"—for them, getting up earlier may be best.

You will need to be flexible to allow your child to take part in some after-school activities. Having a regular homework time doesn't mean that your child will do homework at exactly the same time every day. But every kid alive has said, "I'll do my homework later"; only "later" didn't come—or came so close to bedtime that they couldn't finish their schoolwork. On the other hand, Andrew Ellingsen advised, "Give your child 30 minutes to play after school. Outside is best, but if that's not possible, then dump out the Legos or get out a game they enjoy. They'll concentrate better if they can have a little break."

If you find your child doing homework every night after the time they should be in bed, you may be *too* flexible. And if they are so involved with after-school activities that they don't ever seem to have time for homework, you need to reevaluate the schedule. They might have to drop something so they can be sure to get homework completed.

Do set—and enforce—a rule that there's no screen time until homework is complete. (And yes, by "screen time" you must include Xbox and Minecraft.) If you have one computer and several kids with homework that requires them to be online, you'll have to set a schedule so each child gets a turn.

Find a place to study. Some parents feel that they need to create a Pinterest-ready study area for their child to do homework. They don't. On the other hand, some kids say they can study perfectly well while sitting in front of the TV. They can't.

Finding a place for your child to study is, like so much of parenting, a process of finding the happy medium. All a child needs to do homework is a quiet place, a good light, and relative quiet. The kitchen table works fine. If you have several children, you may want to set up a homework station for each one. In a box or a container that's easy to move, pull together everything they need—markers, sticky notes, planners. Get the box out when it's time for homework; stash it away when the assignments are done. (Just be sure the markers go *back* in the homework box or your child will spend 20 minutes tomorrow wandering around the house looking for the blue and green markers.)

Limit distractions. During study time, turn off the TV. Keep the noise level down. In some families, everyone does something quiet during the study hour—if they aren't doing schoolwork, they are reading a book, finishing some work for the office, or reading for pleasure. If you can't keep the noise level down, you might think about a set of noise-blocking headphones for your student. And some kids really *do* learn better with a little music in the background—but it needs to be quiet and something without a vocal track. Experiment and see. If it takes your child twice as long to do 10 math problems when they are listening to music than when they aren't, then they are someone who needs to study in a quiet spot.

Be close but not too close. Especially as kids are learning how to concentrate on homework, you may need to stay close by. You can check to be sure they are staying on task and not playing an online game. You'll also be available if they have a question about something they don't understand.

Make a daily study plan. Have kids start each session with a study plan. Ask them to write down their goals for that day's study session (or at least tell them to you). Then make sure they have completed those goals before the end of their study session.

Most kids should start with their toughest subject and end with the subject they find the easiest. This is the time when they are most alert. They'll also be relieved when it's finished and can look forward to the rest of their assignments.

Plan for longer-term assignments. Your child's study session will often include some time on a project that is not due the next day. Whether it's studying spelling words for the test on Friday or reading a book for a book report that is due in two weeks, those longer assignments should be broken down into shorter sections so they aren't overwhelming on the night before the due date.

Don't do the work for your child. When kids are struggling with homework, the temptation is to jump in and do it for them. But even though that might solve your immediate problem, it just creates further problems down the road. If they really can't do the work, write a brief note to the teacher explaining what you observed. It may well be that your child doesn't understand the concept that is the focus of the assignment. In that case, the teacher may need to go back and review the content. But if you do the homework and turn it in, your child may not learn the content at all. Since many concepts build on previous learning, this could have far-reaching effects.

Check finished homework. When kids are in elementary school, it's usually a good idea to look over their assignments every day to make sure they are completed. Find out how involved your child's teacher wants you to be. Some teachers want parents to do nothing more than check that the assignments are completed. Others prefer to have parents look over the homework, checking for errors.

67. DO OTHER KIDS DO THEIR BIG PROJECTS AT THE LAST MINUTE? AND HOW CAN I GET MY CHILD TO PLAN AHEAD?

In kindergarten and first grade, most projects last a day or two. But as students move through school, the projects get bigger, the deadlines move further away—and students have that many more opportunities to put things off until the last second.

Which they will. It's a sad fact of life: Kids don't plan ahead. Sooner or later, your child will look up from the dinner table and say, "Did I tell you that I have a history project due tomorrow?"

This will, of course, be the first time you have heard anything about the history project. And while there is very little you can do with *this* big project, you can help your child develop skills so the next big project will go a little more smoothly. Here are three ways to help any child, even the most time-challenged, break down those big projects into smaller, achievable chunks.

Teach backward planning. The science fair isn't for six weeks. To your fifth grader, it might as well be six *years* away. So your job is to help them plan backward. If the plants for their science experiment need to be at least 6 inches high, and if they grow an inch a week, they need to plant them—well, today.

You can teach this skill every time you prepare a meal. Say, "We want to eat dinner at 6:30. The pizza will take 30 minutes to bake. So that means we'd better put it in the oven by 6:00."

Give your child practice planning backward. Say, "You need to be at the bus stop tomorrow by 8:00. Sometimes the bus comes a little early, so you should plan to get there 5 minutes early—at 7:55. It will take you 10 minutes to walk to the bus stop. That means you need to leave the house no later than 7:45. Since it takes you about 5 minutes to gather up your things, you should finish breakfast by 7:40. If you allow 15 minutes to eat breakfast and 20 minutes to get dressed and make your bed, you need to get up no later than 7:05 tomorrow morning."

When that big project comes along, walk your child through the same steps. How many days will it take to make the poster? Write the report? Type the report? Conduct the experiment? Mark backward from the day *before* the science fair. Write each deadline on the calendar.

Take it "bird by bird." My favorite author, Anne Lamott, has told a story about her childhood. Her brother was working on a report on birds. He'd had three months to write it. He'd put it off until the day before it was due:

> He was at the kitchen table close to tears, surrounded by binder paper and pencils and unopened books on birds, immobilized by the hugeness of the task ahead. Then my father sat down beside him, put his arm around my brother's shoulder, and said, "Bird by bird, buddy. Just take it bird by bird."[11]

Whether your child is writing a report on the birds of California or a research paper on the causes of the Civil War, Lamott's advice is exactly what they need. Take that big project and break it down into a series of achievable birds. Er, chunks.

They can't write the paper until they've written an outline. They can't write the outline until they do the research. That requires a trip to the library and then several sessions of reading and taking notes. Step by step, they can get it done.

Keep poster board on hand, just in case. Even if you follow both these pieces of advice, you will inevitably be faced with that last-minute announcement that a big history project is due tomorrow. A quick glance at the clock will confirm that there is no store open within 20 miles of your house. This is the time when you will be glad that you have stashed away a supply of poster board.

Early in the year, buy sheets of poster board in several colors. Put them in a safe place. It must be somewhere your child won't find your supply yet somewhere you will remember it. (Near the washing machine is a place most children will never go. Or put it in the back of your closet.)

There may be families that go through a year without actually using any of their emergency stash of poster board. Personally, I have never met them.

Oh, and one other piece of advice. Unless you are a committed helicopter parent, you do not want this last-minute stuff to become a regular habit. So provide the poster board and the crayons and then turn the project over to your child. "I have already completed the fifth grade" is a good phrase to master on such occasions. Yes, it will be a messy project. Yes, they will be cranky the next day.

But there are two things that are absolutely the truth: First, no one ever was kept out of Harvard because of a messy fifth-grade social studies project. And next time, when you ask, "Would you like to do some planning for that big project?" they'll likely say yes.

68. WHAT IF MY CHILD SAYS THEY DON'T HAVE ANY HOMEWORK?

After "I'll do it later," the next most popular way for kids to avoid doing homework is to say they don't have any. And sometimes, that may even be true.

Perhaps you are working to create a system for keeping track of assignments, but it is still, shall we say, a work in progress. In fact, this problem crops up often enough that many schools make it easy for parents to find out about the day's assignments. They set up a homework hotline for parents to call or help teachers create individual homework pages on the school website. After a quick check, you can say, "Actually, Mr. Jacobs's website says you have 15 math problems due tomorrow."

If there really is nothing due for tomorrow, your child can get a jump start on a longer-term project. They can read a chapter in their book report book or do some online research for a history project. If they have a test coming up, time spent studying now will pay off in the future.

And since you are trying to help your child develop a homework *habit*, you should set aside time every night for some learning-related activity. They can review spelling words. They can do a few extra math problems. Or they can spend some time reading about a subject that interests them, even if it is not for a school assignment.

69. HOW DOES A PARENT'S ROLE IN HOMEWORK CHANGE DURING MIDDLE AND HIGH SCHOOL?

The two realities for homework in middle and high school: There will be more of it, and you will probably understand less of it. Your teen may be studying a language you can't speak. Their math class may move well beyond any math you remember.

But that doesn't mean you get to wish your teen luck and tell them you'll see them at graduation. There's still a role for you to play when your teen moves into middle and high school.

Know your role. You need to back off from daily homework involvement since too much parental involvement in middle school can actually be harmful. The best way to help is by monitoring your teen's study habits and by helping them develop better habits. You should also continue to talk about homework—if they are struggling most of the time, you'll want to reach out to their teachers to develop a plan of action. If an assignment comes back with comments by the teacher, take a look at those. You'll get a better idea of whether your teen understands the material.

By the high school years, your teen should be largely in charge of homework. By this point, it's their responsibility. You can act as a sounding board, letting them talk about issues or concerns. You can work with them to break down larger projects into smaller, more manageable steps. And you can share with them your strategies for remaining organized. But under no circumstances should you *ever* do your teen's homework. Don't write the paper. Don't finish the math problems. Don't do the online research for the history project. Unless you're planning to do all those things when your teen goes to college (and there are some parents who do), then it's time to back out of the homework process as much as you can.

Scheduling homework time is critical. According to the National Center for Education Statistics, the typical teen spends about 7.5 hours per week on homework.[12] When homework time is combined with time spent in after-school activities or part-time jobs, it's hard to fit everything in. Here are some tips on how to make sure there's enough time for homework:

- Start by blocking out time that's already committed. If they have basketball practice from 3:00 to 6:00, they can't work on their science project then. But after school, sports, and other activities are blocked in, there should still be plenty of time available for homework.

- Write down when major assignments and tests are due. Crisis cramming doesn't work, so it's important to set aside time over several days to review and prepare for a test.
- Use smaller bits of time. If your teen is studying a second language, spending 10 minutes a day can help them memorize new vocabulary.
- Try the "pomodoro" technique to maintain focus. (The name comes from the tomato-shaped timer that the person who invented this approach used.) Choose one thing to focus on. Set a timer for 25 minutes. During that time, work only on the focus area—no checking text messages, no wandering over to YouTube. When the 25 minutes are up, take a 5-minute break. This technique is easy to learn. It can result in real gains in productivity. (It's also how this book got finished.)

70. MY TEEN WANTS TO LISTEN TO MUSIC AND TEXT WITH FRIENDS WHEN THEY STUDY. THEY SAY IT'S "MULTITASKING" AND THAT ADULTS DO IT ALL THE TIME. WHAT DOES THE RESEARCH SAY?

I woke up on the morning I was going to write this answer with multitasking, obviously, on my brain. Before I sat down at the computer, I decided to do a little multitasking of my own. I put a coffee pod in the coffeepot and pushed the button. Then I started loading dishes in the dishwasher. I was feeling very efficient.

Until I turned around and realized that while I had pushed the button on the coffee maker, I hadn't actually put my coffee mug under the spigot. So instead of drinking my coffee, I had to clean it up from the counter and the floor. In trying to do two things at once, I hadn't done either of them very well.

Teens often tell parents they can multitask while they are studying. They really believe it's fine for them to send text messages to two or three friends, chat online with another, catch up on last night's TV show . . . *and* do their homework at the same time.

Researchers sometimes call this behavior *media multitasking* (MM), and it's definitely on the rise. It's now so prevalent (nearly a third of adolescents use task-related and task-unrelated media "most of the time" while studying)[13] that students as young as middle school try to convince their parents that MM will not affect their homework.

And boy, would it be nice if brains would allow us to do all those things at the same time. But the fact is that, mostly, our brains are just not wired to do it very well. In fact, MM leads to all of the following:

- problems staying focused;
- inability to switch tasks;
- lesser growth mindset;
- increased distractibility; and
- lower impulse control.[14]

Homework, in particular, is something that requires concentration and focus. Every time a student switches attention from math to, say, an online argument between two friends, it will take some time to return the focus to the math problem. The American Psychological Association has offered this trenchant observation: "Psychologists tend to liken the job [of switching focus back and forth] to choreography or air-traffic control, noting that in these operations, as in others, mental overload can result in catastrophe."[15]

Some students can do their homework while listening to music, but only if it's instrumental music and not songs with words. And of course, texting with four friends is not a good way to keep a focus on Spanish verb tenses.

Now, there are some tasks that are suitable for multitasking, although no kid I ever knew is going to be happy to hear this. Lawn work—weeding, mowing, raking—is fairly repetitive and can easily provide time to simultaneously think through the organization for a paper. A poet friend said that washing dishes had the same effect for her. She'd sometimes go into what she called her "poet trance," coming out of it much later with her hands in cold dishwater but a fully formed poem in her brain.

Neither of those tasks is likely to appeal to your teen, of course. But they might try listening to an assigned book on tape while they are exercising. They could review their Spanish vocabulary while walking to the bus stop.

The lure of multitasking argues that right through middle and high school, students should do their homework somewhere you can at least keep an eye on them. You'll know whether they're really working on history homework . . . or TikTok videos. And a casual check-in every now and then will also give them a chance to ask a question or talk about a problem.

71. MY TEEN IS STRUGGLING TO COMPLETE A HOMEWORK ASSIGNMENT. HOW CAN I HELP?

Your teen is struggling with their homework in physics, a subject you took decades ago. (And possibly didn't like even then.) They're trying to conjugate Spanish verbs, but you studied French in school.

Nearly every parent comes to a point when they have to admit that they just don't understand their teen's homework. When the National Center for Family Literacy surveyed parents, nearly half said they were struggling to help their child with homework. Nearly as many—46.5%—admitted that they didn't understand the subject matter.[16]

If you find yourself in this position, it's best just to be honest from the start. Say something like, "I don't understand this either. Let's see what we *do* know about this subject and if we can figure it out."

Let them know that homework is still important and that you're impressed by the work they're doing. And remind them that the purpose of homework is to learn. Then have your teen explain to you what they do understand. For example, if they're trying to solve a math problem, have them tell you the steps they should follow. It may be that they suddenly realize they've left out a step—"Oh, I need to multiply and divide *before* I add and subtract."

They should also see if there's any more information in the textbook. Sometimes, there will be a sample problem that can help your teen see the process they should follow to solve the problem. Or ask if they've ever done any problem like the one that has flummoxed them now. Often, new knowledge builds on something your teen has already studied. Perhaps by looking back at the earlier problem, this one will become clear.

Make sure they have everything they need to do the assignment. One mother finally figured out why her son was struggling in Spanish. Yes, he owned a Spanish dictionary, but he kept it in his bedroom while he did his homework in the kitchen. Since he didn't want to walk "all that way" to look up a word he didn't understand, he just kept guessing. Once the dictionary was close at hand, his ability to translate Spanish improved dramatically!

Finally, if they are still struggling, have them write a short note or email to the teacher, outlining what they tried and where they went off track. This will help the teacher figure out how to help them understand the material.

72. THERE WAS A TIME WHEN EVERY TEACHER TALKED ABOUT LEARNING STYLES (AUDITORY, VISUAL, KINESTHETIC). BUT NOW TEACHERS DON'T SEEM TO TALK ABOUT IT AS MUCH. AS A PARENT, WHAT DO I NEED TO KNOW ABOUT MY CHILD'S LEARNING STYLE?

Here's a case where the latest brain research is helping us *unlearn* some things we thought were true. For years, teachers and parents believed that children had a distinct learning style. Typically, these learning styles were designated visual, auditory, and kinesthetic. The belief was that children would learn best only if information was presented in a way that matched that learning preference. So teachers spent hours and hours trying to figure out a kinesthetic way to teach, for example, the *ch* sound.

Now we know the research didn't hold up. The studies that first identified these learning styles were not based on very good science. And when researchers tried to replicate the findings using the best research methods, they couldn't.

It's true that most people do have a preference for a way to receive information. There are people who learn best when they hear things, or see things, or learn while moving. But there's no evidence, even after many studies, that people learn *better* if that's the way they receive their information.[17]

Daniel Willingham, a professor of psychology at the University of Virginia, summarized the research on learning styles in a *New York Times* editorial with the wonderful title "Are You a Visual or an Auditory Learner? It Doesn't Matter." His advice was that instead of trying to transform a task to meet your particular learning style, "transform your thinking to match the task. The best strategy for a task is the best strategy, irrespective of what you believe your learning style is."[18]

Good teachers who understand the learning goals of their lesson have *always* tried to change up how they present the information. There's nothing like a hands-on chemistry experiment to help students understand a chemical reaction—when the material in the test tube suddenly changes color or bubbles out of the tube.

But sometimes, there's really only one best strategy. Foreign languages just have to include auditory teaching. Only when students hear how the *rr* sound is pronounced in Spanish can they re-create it correctly.

Students are more successful if they use the study method that best matches the content. (You can draw diagrams all day and you'll never learn how to make the *rr* sound.) "Everyone is able to think in words; everyone is able to think in mental images," Willingham said. "It's much better to think of everyone having a toolbox of ways to think, and think to yourself, which tool is best?"[19]

73. CAN KIDS LEARN TO BE SMART?

Many children—and their parents—believe that success in school is largely the result of ability. Kids who are smart, they believe, will automatically do well in school. And children who do poorly in one or more subjects often write off their disappointing performance by saying something like, "I'm just not good in math."

Yet those same students will approach other activities with the confidence that they can and will improve. Like Michael Jordan, they know they will get better at shooting free throws if they practice. They don't expect to shoot free throws in basketball without practice. They wouldn't plan to swim the butterfly without coaching and hours in the pool. But academics? They figure kids are either born smart or they aren't.

Of course, brain researchers know that isn't true. There's scientific evidence that the neural connections in our brains grow and become stronger the more we struggle with learning and overcome our mistakes. In fact, researchers at Stanford University now have evidence that students who develop what they call a *growth mindset* have higher levels of success in school than those who don't. "A growth mindset," said Stanford professor Carol Dweck who coined the term based on her research, "is when students believe that their abilities can be developed. . . .

"We found that if we changed students' mindsets, we could boost their achievement," Dweck wrote in *Education Week*. "More precisely, students who believed their intelligence could be developed (a growth mindset) outperformed those who believed their intelligence was fixed (a fixed mindset)."[20]

Certainly, talent plays a role in achievement. But research studying geniuses or people who have made great creative contributions to their fields is showing us that talent *alone* does not explain success. Instead, the thing that seems to set the high achievers apart from others is the hours they spend focusing on improving their performance.[21] These high achievers develop their expertise over time and as a result of focused effort. All of that is fostered by a growth mindset.

When children believe that intelligence is fixed, they will identify themselves as "smart" or "not smart." Rather than seeing mistakes as a sign that they may need to work a little harder, they will see mistakes as evidence of a lack of inherent capability and may give up rather than have others see them as "stupid" or incapable. On the other hand, children with a growth mindset will be more likely to seek help when something gets in their way, believing the capability is in them, but they just need a hand to find it.

Model a growth mindset yourself. Try learning something new—whether it's a skill you need for your job or something you want to learn for your own enjoyment. Don't hide the challenges you face from your child. Acknowledge that you still have work to do, but that you're sure if you keep at it, you can get better.

Developing a "yet sensibility." In their book *Neuro Teach: Brain Science and the Future of Education*, Glenn Whitman and Ian Kelleher called this a *yet sensibility*, and they said it's key to helping students develop a growth mindset.[22] The key word in helping kids develop a growth mindset is *yet*. When kids are stuck, they often feel like they'll never get unstuck. That's when parents need to step in. Reframe their thinking from "I can't do this" to "I can't do this *yet*."

As Whitman and Kelleher said, "We know that developing a growth mindset, or 'yet sensibility' in each child is critical as he or she faces those inevitable academic, social, and emotional bumps in the road that all students meet through their academic journey, and that all children face in their lives outside school as they grow up."[23]

So when they say they can't ride a bike, answer, "Well, you can't ride it *yet*. But keep at it and you'll master it." And when they're frustrated because they can't solve for x? The response is the same: "You can't do it *yet*." When you take this attitude, you give kids the confidence that you know they will solve the problem. It's not that you're "not good in math." It's that you're "not good in math *yet*."

One way to help develop a growth mindset is by explicitly helping students see the link between their effort and their achievement. Here's a sample rubric that might help:

Table 8.1.   Effort and Achievement Rubric

Effort Rubric		Achievement Rubric	
4	I worked on my assignment in _____ until it was completed. Even when difficulties arose, I kept working on the task. I didn't give up when a solution was not immediately clear. I treated obstacles as opportunities—I used obstacles that arose as opportunities to strengthen my understanding and skills beyond the minimum required to complete the assignment.	I exceeded the objectives of the assignment. (I could teach others how to do this.)	4
3	I worked on my _____ assignment until it was completed. I pushed myself to continue working on the task even when difficulties arose, when a solution was not immediately apparent, or when I had trouble understanding what an author was saying.	I met the objectives of the assignment. (I can do this on my own now.)	3
2	I put some effort into my _____ assignment, but I stopped working when difficulties arose, when a solution was not immediately evident, or when I had trouble understanding what an author was saying.	I met a few of the objectives of the assignment, but didn't meet others. (I still need help with this.)	2
1	I put very little effort into my _____ assignment.	I did not meet the objectives of the assignment. (I don't understand this.)	1

Scale: 4 = excellent; 3 = good; 2 = needs improvement; 1 = unacceptable

74. WHAT'S THE BEST WAY TO STUDY FOR A TEST?

From a first-grade spelling test to a high school Advanced Placement exam, tests are a fact of life for students. And just as students can learn and master the times tables or the conjugation of the Spanish verb *ser*, they can also learn and master the skills they need to study more successfully for a test.

Make a plan. Help your child think about how much time it's likely to take to be prepared for the test. Obviously, a plan for a spelling test will be different from the plan for a final exam in history. If they're studying for a spelling test, set aside 10 or 15 minutes each night to practice spelling. But if it's a year-end test, it may take several weeks of reviewing and preparation.

Practice makes perfect . . . but when *you practice is important.* Whenever our brains are learning something new—whether it's a set of facts, a new skill, or a complex procedure—it usually takes more than one try before we remember it. Now brain researchers have learned that it's not just the practice, but when the practice happens that affects long-term retention.

A brain researcher from Dartmouth explored the best way to help students remember what they've learned. His research showed that something called *spaced repetition* produces the greatest return.[24] A student who spends 10 minutes a day reviewing Spanish vocabulary words will probably remember more of them than the student who tried to learn them all in the hour before the test. At least one study found that students with higher GPAs are more likely to space out their study.[25]

This research confirms that the most important guidance you can give your child: Cramming the night before a test doesn't work. Several shorter study periods, spread over several days, are better than one last-minute cram session.

Test yourself. It turns out that one of the best ways to overcome a case of testing nerves is . . . by doing more testing. But frequent practice tests are one of the fastest ways to improve memory and retention.[26] When you answer a test question, you have to search through your brain's long-term memory. That creates more and better pathways to the answer, which in turn makes it easier to come up with the answer the next time you see it on, say, a test.

It's called *retrieval practice*, and along with spaced repetition these two strategies turn out to be two of the best ways to commit things to your long-term memory. It's not hard to create a practice test—a set of flash cards are an easy way to review information. So is turning to those questions at the end of the chapter.

But it's important to be sure you are practicing the correct answer. As a parent, you can help—ask a question from the flash cards, check the answer, and then be sure it's correct. As legendary football coach Vince Lombardi used to say, "Practice does not make perfect. Only perfect practice makes perfect."

For a big and really important exam—for example, an AP test—your teen needs to take the same kind of test that they will take for credit. If it's an essay test that has to be completed in 45 minutes, then that's the best kind of practice test. Students can often find copies of old exams online.

Change up the study style. Staring at a textbook for hours is *one* way to review for a test. But it's not the best way. Instead, help your child come up with some more active approaches. Make flash cards and review them. Have your child act out a scene from history or create a rap about the elements in the periodic table.

Try interleaving. Don't just have your student change up their study style. Encourage them to switch to a different topic or subject every hour or so. Rather than focusing on one topic for hours, interleaving will actually improve memory. In addition, having some variation will make it easier for them to pay attention longer.

Take breaks. It's also important to encourage your student to break up their studying with smart breaks. Taking a 15-minute break once every hour can work wonders on keeping them focused and productive.

Good studying starts in school. Taking notes in class is a good way to help students focus on what the teacher is saying. Reviewing those notes as soon as possible after class will help cement the new learning.

Homework and study skills are really not optional for students. They are the way to reinforce what the teacher is teaching in the classroom. So your job as a parent is to work with your child to develop the best way to study.

You should support them as they do the work. Help them carve out time to study. If possible, find a quiet place (or at least some noise-canceling headphones).

Support your child in other ways. Ask the spelling words. Quiz them on math facts. Schedule a trip to the store to buy poster board.

But on the other hand, you already went to fifth grade. So it should be your fifth grader, and not you, who does the homework. Which is likely to be beyond your skills by the time your kid gets into middle or high school anyway.

9

WHAT PARENTS SHOULD ASK ABOUT BECOMING ADVOCATES FOR CHANGE

It always seems impossible until it's done.

—Nelson Mandela

It is the rare parent who never wants to change anything about the way their child is educated. The good news is that you often can. But the bad news is that if you use the wrong approach—and there are some spectacularly wrong approaches—you can screw things up not only for your child but for every other kid in the district.

On the other hand, you can actually change things for every student in the district if your advocacy is successful. And while going to meetings and collecting documentation is not as instantly rewarding as posting some zinger on a Facebook mom group chat, it can have a more lasting impact.

The process of advocating for one child or for many actually follows the same step-by-step approach.

First, understand the chain of command. Schools and school districts are top-down organizations. Parents who are most successful in getting things done understand and use that structure. "You have to follow the stair steps," said Janet Soller, who not only earned a PhD in education but is also the mother of five boys. "You can't skip a step or you'll likely just have to go back and do it over."

School governance in this country is intentionally set up to be decentralized. There are some decisions that can only be made at the local level, for example. It's best if you understand that while no, your teacher can't change IDEA—the federal law governing education for children with disabilities—neither can your U.S. senator revise the amount of money allocated to the swim and dive program in your local school district budget.

But in most cases, it's best to start by talking to the teacher. Then move up to the principal, the district office, the superintendent, and the school board. The lower the level, the closer to your child, so the easier it probably will be to get a change made.

Second, keep records. Things don't always work out after one meeting. So put things in writing. After a conference with the teacher, you might say, "I'll send you an email with my understanding of this plan. That way we will both have a record."

These notes will help if you need to move up to the next level. "Charlie's teacher, Ms. Jackson, says she can't make a decision to have him tested for the gifted program, but that you as the principal could do that." You may learn that Charlie's teacher was simply engaging in the age-old practice of kicking the can down the road and that she can in fact recommend him for testing. Or you may learn that it is a school decision. But in either case, you're more likely to get Charlie tested.

A comprehensive set of notes will also be invaluable if your work to change policy stretches over several months. Memories fade, but a good memo to the files will last forever.

Third, and perhaps most important, don't get angry. You may be frustrated. You may in fact feel furious. But any policy maker will tell you that anger is the least persuasive tool to convince them to change their mind. It makes it too easy to dismiss you and thus your concerns.

So practice your Lamaze breathing or take along a friend who will pinch you under the table if you start to lose it. Stay calm, and you have a much better chance of walking out of the room with the outcome you desire.

75. MY CHILD IS HAVING A PROBLEM WITH A TEACHER. WHAT SHOULD I DO?

Actually, this answer is pretty self-evident. If you have a problem with a teacher, *talk* to the teacher.

It's not hard to understand why parents want to avoid this step. It obviously can be uncomfortable. You may worry that the conversation will somehow affect how the teacher treats your kid. But you aren't going to get anywhere until you tackle this head-on.

When you reach the principal, the first question you'll be asked is, "Have you talked with the teacher?" Many won't meet with you until that's done.

Ask for the meeting by email—both you and the teacher will have a record of the request. Especially if you tend to get emotional (and we all do when our kids are concerned), a written request will let you edit some of the emotion out. And if things head south later, you have at least started the paper trail.

As clearly as you can, spell out the reasons you are asking for a meeting. "I am concerned about Ava's math grades this year," or "I would like to talk to you about the way the school addressed a fight on the playground last week." Giving the teacher a heads-up means they will be able to bring the documentation they need to answer your question.

Try not to see the teacher as an enemy. Teachers really do go into education because they want kids to learn. So start from the perspective that you and the teacher likely want the same thing, which is for your child to learn something in the class.

Find something positive to say as the meeting starts. "Jessica especially enjoyed the chance to read the *Boxcar Children* books." Remember—your goal is to get the teacher to see your point of view. You are not likely to do that if you take an adversarial approach from the beginning. (Most teachers will also take this approach, so at least for the first 5 minutes of the conversation, you can have a pleasant exchange.)

Stay positive as long as you can. "You do not want to make the teacher look foolish," Soller advised. "You do not want to embarrass the teacher."

One tip from me: Don't assume you know the whole story. It's quite possible that neither you *nor* the teacher fully knows what's going on. One teacher I know always told parents, "I won't believe everything I hear about *you* if you will promise not to believe everything your child tells you about *me*."

You may be shocked to learn this, but children can often be described by a term familiar to fiction readers: They can be *unreliable narrators*. Children are never entirely objective about situations where they are personally involved. Even if your child has told you that they *did* turn in all their homework, but the teacher lost it, accept the possibility that your child might be trying to portray the situation in a better light than the facts would actually warrant.

In her fifth-grade year, my daughter Sara had received a grade of C in social studies during the first marking period. Her explanation—that the teacher was boring/capricious/unfair/picking on her—didn't really hold water, but I was concerned enough to make an appointment to see the teacher. She opened the grade book and showed me that Sara had never handed in several assignments. It turned out that the C grade was pretty much a gift.

I was certainly glad I had approached this conversation as a fact-finding exercise rather than a search-and-destroy mission. And later, at home, Sara and I had a serious conversation about meeting responsibilities. (This mostly consisted of me repeating a variation of "I don't care if you don't like her; you have to turn in your work.") She buckled down and, eventually, the teacher became one of her favorites.

Ask to see samples of your child's work. Discuss these examples of your child's work with the teacher. If you are going to ask for your child to be tested for special services, whether because of a learning disability or because you believe your child is gifted, get a copy (use your phone to take a photo if necessary) of the assignments the teacher has selected. If you are concerned about a low grade, ask if you could see samples of student work that earned a high grade (many teachers will share samples, although they may block out the name of the student who did it). Sometimes, there are simple things your child can correct—checking over a book report one last time, rewriting an essay after carefully editing it.

Try to keep the focus on problem solving. See if you and the teacher can work out a plan to address the problem that brought you to school. And be sure to thank the teacher for taking time to meet with you.

When it's time to call the teacher

Parents sometimes worry that they should not be bothering the teacher with a concern. Maybe, they think, things will just work out.

That can happen. It's why it's not a good idea to call the school every time your child grumbles about something that went on in school. But there are times when a call to the teacher is warranted. Here are five times when you should definitely contact the teacher:

1. There's a big change in your child's behavior. Your formerly happy-go-lucky child is suddenly withdrawn and anxious. Your kid who couldn't wait to go to school has started crying at breakfast.
2. There is a big change in their grades. It may be in one subject or in all of them, but if you see any major drop in grades

(more than one letter grade), that's a signal that something is going on.

3. You start to suspect that what you're hearing from your child is not true. They say they are all caught up in science, but other parents are talking about a big science notebook that's due next week. They say the math teacher never gives homework, but other parents are talking about making flash cards.

4. Your child is struggling consistently with doing homework. They are frustrated and say they just don't understand.

5. There's a change in what's going on at home that may be affecting how your child is acting at school. Even happy events like a new baby can affect school performance.

76. I DON'T THINK THE SCHOOL HAS THE SAME EXPECTATIONS FOR MY BLACK SON AS THEY HAVE FOR WHITE STUDENTS. WHAT DO I DO?

If you are concerned that a teacher may not have high expectations for your child (something parents of color have told me they often have to deal with), a face-to-face meeting can often create a clear understanding. A friend went to see her daughter's algebra teacher at the end of the first marking period in the ninth grade. The teacher initially seemed unconcerned about the C grade she had given to my friend's Black daughter. "A C isn't a bad grade," the teacher said.

"It is at *my* house," my friend replied.

Be persistent. Remember Jonathan Amaya's story of scheduling himself into an upper-level math class. Jonathan kept at it and eventually got registered for the class—and went on to earn a full scholarship and receive a degree in engineering. But it all could have stopped in that counselor's office.

A conversation with the teacher or the school is one critical way you can share your views and values about achievement and expectations. Do it as early in the year as you can.

Teachers, like everyone else, grew up with a worldview that has been infused by unconscious racism. Often, as they think they are simply removing pressure from a student, they are actually conveying the impression that the child can't be expected to excel. And that leads them unconsciously to lower their expectations for students of color.

Research has confirmed that teacher expectations are a critical link in student achievement. Researchers at Clemson University tracked teacher expectations of more than 20,000 students from kindergarten through Grade 8. They found that math teachers held lower expectations for white girls and for students of color. And, you will not be surprised to learn, the students who were not *expected* to do well did in fact not do as well.

According to Faiza Jamil, who led the research team, the impact of lower teacher expectations continued even after students no longer had that teacher—in fact, low teacher expectations predicted low achievement as long as three years into the future.[1]

Still, the study also held out some hope. Teachers who held *higher* expectations for students could have the same impact, even several years down the road. So the lesson for teachers is to raise expectations for all students, and the lesson for parents is to make sure the school knows that's what you want for your child.

77. I MET WITH THE TEACHER. NOTHING HAS CHANGED. WHAT DO I DO NEXT?

There are sometimes issues that can't be resolved with the teacher, or that the teacher could, but will not, address. So the next step is to talk to the principal (or, in a large school, an assistant principal).

Yes, for most of us, a visit to the principal's office still makes us nervous. But there are some problems that only an administrator can resolve.

Perhaps you have tried to work with the teacher, but your child is still struggling. That may be time to request a different teacher or a transfer to a different class. Perhaps your child is experiencing a problem in most or all of their classes. Bullying, for example, is often something that occurs most frequently when students are *out* of class in places like the hallway, the cafeteria, the locker room, or the restroom.

Use much of the advice on planning a successful parent–teacher meeting. Request an appointment in writing. Call to follow up—and tell the school secretary why you are asking for the meeting.

Bring your documentation with you. If you have had meetings with one or more teachers, have the date and time of the meeting, as well as any written follow-up, available to show the principal.

You may also need to up your game in other ways. Soller passed along advice from Sally Smith, the founder of Washington's Lab School, which served children with disabilities: Show up with a man who is wearing a suit. "She used to say the man didn't even have to say anything," Soller recalled. "But a man in a suit does seem to move the needle."

Here are some other things to keep in mind when you talk with the principal:

- You are the expert on your son or daughter. That gives you an important voice in the conversation. Your point of view won't be the only one heard, but you are a key player in the meeting.
- The principal has to look at the impact of any decision on the entire school. If the principal allows one student to break the rules, they're going to have to let every student do the same.
- Documentation helps. Did your child come home with a black eye after a student assaulted them at the bus stop? Take a picture. Did a teacher send you an unprofessional email? Bring a copy.
- Don't be afraid to ask for what you want. Would you like your daughter moved to another algebra section? Would you like your son to eat lunch at a different time? Are you asking that your child be tested to see if they qualify for special education? It will be easier for the school administration to resolve the problem if they have an idea of what you want.
- On the other hand, don't expect special favors. Principals won't (or anyway, shouldn't) change a grade that a teacher has given. They can't overlook the fact that your senior brought alcohol on the band trip or pulled the fire alarm.

By the time parents reach the principal, they are often frustrated. But as a former Fairfax County assistant principal said, it's important to view the principal as someone who wants to be your ally. "I think the bottom line is we are partners in this together. I can't tell you the number of parents who come with their metaphorical guns loaded—maybe because they had a bad experience somewhere else. I want to say, 'You don't need the hostile attitude. We really want to do what's best for your kid.'"

For the record, that statement should probably be rated as mostly true. Or perhaps true for most administrators. There are some you won't be able to work with—and for them, you need to read the answer to Question 79.

78. CAN I ASK FOR MY CHILD TO
BE ASSIGNED TO A SPECIFIC TEACHER?

Any woman knows that an article of clothing marked "one size fits all" just doesn't. Often, a teacher who has a great rapport with one child may not be as successful with a child who learns differently.

That's why parents sometimes worry as one school year draws to a close. If their child has had a good year, they worry whether some of that progress could be lost with a different kind of teacher. If their child has had a miserable year, they want to know what to do to make the next year better.

In some schools, savvy parents simply called the principal and requested a particular teacher. While that approach worked for the kids whose parents knew how to work the system, other kids often got stuck with the teachers no one had requested. Or schools ended up with 55 requests for one teacher, with 30 disappointed parents on the day class lists were posted.

So today, most schools have a "no request" policy. But here's the good news: You can still ask for a teacher—if you know how.

The key is to give principals information about your child and how they learn best. Rather than asking for a teacher by name, describe the environment in which your child has been most—and least—successful. Here are some tips:

- Plan ahead. Write your letter near the end of the school year. If you wait until mid- or late summer, principals may have class assignments nearly completed.
- Be honest about your child's strengths and weaknesses. A child with attention issues will do better in a classroom with a little more structure. A child who lacks self-confidence may be more successful with a teacher who is nurturing. Principals who are making class assignments want to know information like this—they truly do want to help all children have a successful year.
- Describe the kind of personality that works best with your child. A shy child may be hurt by humor that another child would find hilarious.
- Especially if your child has not had a successful year, resist the urge to play the blame game. You may need to write two or three drafts of your letter, but try to make it as objective as possible. Instead of saying, "I've heard Mr. X is terrible and I don't want my child in

his class," try to cast things in a positive light. If the principal feels defensive when reading your letter, you're much less likely to get the outcome you want.

Letters requesting a teacher

Here's the kind of letter you should write if your child has had a good year:

Dear Dr. Jones,

As the school year draws to a close, I want to thank you and all the teachers here at Bright Day Elementary School.

This year has been an especially productive one for Jacob. He has made great progress in reading (more than 1.5 years, according to his teacher Ms. Jackson). His math scores are now on grade level. He comes home happy and proud of what he has accomplished.

I give Ms. Jackson enormous credit for that success. Her classroom is quiet, orderly, and structured. The children know the boundaries and feel free to explore and grow in a safe environment within them. Clearly, it has been good for Jacob.

As you know, Jacob is enthusiastic. But sometimes, his enthusiasm can spill over into unruly behavior.

Unfortunately, in an unstructured classroom, Jacob tends to waste time and create distractions for himself and (sometimes) others. After a year in a very unstructured classroom, Jacob entered the third grade this year below grade level in both math and reading.

That's why I am asking you to think about his placement for next year. I hope you will place Jacob with a teacher who provides structure and predictability in their classroom. I know that will allow Jacob to continue to make the kind of progress we have seen this year.

As always, we are available to assist you or any of the teachers at the school in any way we can. Thank you for everything you have done for our children.

Sincerely,
Jacob's mother

Here's the kind of letter to write if your child's year was not as successful:

Dear Dr. Jones,

As the school year is drawing to a close, I want to request your help for the coming year. This has not been a productive year for our son Jacob, and I am asking for your consideration as you make teacher assignments for next year.

As you know, Jacob is enthusiastic. But sometimes, his enthusiasm spills over into unruly behavior. Unfortunately, in an unstructured classroom, Jacob tends to waste time and create distractions for himself and (sometimes) for others.

Sadly, that has been the case this year. Although he entered the second grade reading on grade level, his latest standardized test scores show that he is still reading on the 2.0 level. That means he will face special challenges in third grade. His math scores are similar.

We know that Jacob has not been an easy student to have in class. Ms. Jones has frequently called us to ask for our help in controlling Jacob's behavior.

After several home interventions that had little effect, I came to school and spent a day observing Jacob. I noticed something striking. In Ms. Jones's class, Jacob's attention wandered. But when the students went to music class, where Mr. Englin runs a more structured and predictable class, Jacob's attention never wavered.

I am willing to continue to work with Jacob on behavior issues. But I hope that during the coming year, we might ask for a more structured classroom environment.

Thank you in advance for considering our request. Like you, we want Jacob to do his very best in academics and behavior.

As always, we are available to assist you or any of the teachers at the school in any way we can. Thank you for everything you have done for our children.

Sincerely,
Jacob's mother

Note that the mother is not asking for a specific teacher—a request that is usually a nonstarter. She's also not asking for Jacob to be in a class with his best friend. She's outlining a kind of classroom environment that will allow her child to thrive.

It's not requesting a specific teacher. But it is likely to make sure your child ends up in a classroom that helps them grow and learn.

79. THE PRINCIPAL SAYS THEY CAN'T CHANGE THE POLICY. HOW CAN PARENTS CHANGE DISTRICT POLICIES?

Some issues go beyond what anyone at the school level can do. If you have a concern over a school district policy, then you have to have it addressed at the district level.

Largely, those will be decisions governed either by the district's policies, which are adopted in public meetings and available online, or the school budget, which is also adopted in a public meeting and available online.

Here are some of the issues that would need to be taken up at the school district level:

- Discipline issues. Starting in the 1990s, many school districts adopted "zero tolerance" policies. Typically, they imposed serious punishment for any student who committed an offense related to a weapon, drugs, or certain behavioral issues. Sometimes districts can be persuaded to change these policies. But often it will require a comprehensive review of how the policy is affecting students. If parents can demonstrate, for example, that a particular discipline policy has a disproportionate impact on students of color, they have solid grounds for pushing for a change.
- The school budget. You and other parents may feel that class sizes are too large. The school budget drives that decision. You may want the school to start a new varsity sports team. Again, the district budget will drive that decision.
- Issues that affect many schools. For example, changing the starting time at one high school would involve changes in bus schedules, which in turn would lead to changes in starting times for elementary or middle schools. Only by changing starting times throughout the

district could you achieve the goal of getting high schools to start later.

- Decisions you believe were wrongly decided at the school level.

The bigger the district, the harder it can be to get a policy overturned. But here's how you do it.

Start by reading the policy, or the budget line item, in question. These are public documents, and they are very likely available online. Knowledge is power, and you want to walk into any meeting with a clear understanding of what you want changed.

Reach out to other parents. Surely you're not the only parent whose kid is a zombie because they have to catch the school bus at 6:15 a.m. Use social media and groups like Facebook parent groups to see who else shares your concerns. As the African proverb has it, "If you want to go fast, go alone. If you want to go far, go together." When you are launching an effort that will help a lot of students, it's best to involve as many people as you can.

Do your research. What do other schools or districts do? Are there models that your district could support? Are there costs associated with the changes you are proposing? How could this effort be funded?

Working with other parents, write a clear but short description of what you want to change. Go back to the social media channels and let people know this is what you are doing. More people will likely join you.

You'll want to talk to the policy makers in person. So set up meetings with the school board members and the superintendent or their designee. Follow the basic rule of all school meetings: Don't get mad.

It's possible that a board member will offer to raise the issue at a future meeting. But it's more likely that they will ask to study the issue. They may want to set up a study committee. This is a positive sign, because it means they're considering your proposal seriously. Work with the committee and ask to serve as a member.

Finally, your issue may come to the board for a vote. If so, you'll want to be sure other parents are there. If there is time for public testimony, be sure your side is represented. Sometimes, parents all wear the same color to show their support for your issue.

Is there one parent who can take responsibility for working with the press? They should alert reporters that the issue is coming before the board. You should designate one person—perhaps yourself—to speak on behalf of your group. You don't need a muddy message.

Afterward, win or lose, thank everyone who helped you. Also reach out to those who did not support you this time. If the issue is relevant, it may come up again and perhaps next time they could be talked into supporting your position.

Here's an example of how this can work. A group of parents in Fairfax County wanted to change the district's grading policy. The district's grading scale, which had not changed for 25 years, used a 6-point scale (A = 94–100).

Parents who were concerned about the competitiveness of Fairfax County students in college admissions began to study the impact of this grading scale. They learned that most other districts had changed their grading scale to a 10-point scale, with an A being awarded for any grade from 90 to 100.

This worried parents, especially those whose children were applying to colleges out of state. While most Virginia colleges understood that an A in Fairfax was harder to earn than an A in most other districts, parents were concerned that out-of-state admissions officers would not know that. Thus, a student who would have a 3.5 GPA or higher in some school districts might have a 3.0 in Fairfax.

A group of parents formed an organization they called Fairgrade (this was Fairfax County, after all). The organizers included lawyers, psychologists, a former admissions officer, and a communications strategist who specialized in making television commercials.

The superintendent's initial response to parents was to recommend continuation of the existing grading policy. The parents then asked the school system to set up a committee to study the issue.

After that committee's report came in, the school board adopted the group's recommendation. Fairfax now uses a 10-point grading scale.

The biggest lesson to draw from the Fairgrade example: Persistence can win. When the board and the superintendent offered a study committee instead of a policy change, they agreed. They worked within the limits laid out by the system, and eventually they won.

80. IT'S NOT THE DISTRICT—IT'S THE STATE LAW. HOW CAN PARENTS GET A STATE LAW CHANGED?

"There ought to be a law." That sentiment (or sometimes its reverse: there ought never to be this law) can be a powerful driver for change.

The process of changing a law, however, is not for the faint of heart. Here's a typical time line:

- A bill is introduced in at least one chamber of the legislature.
- It is assigned to a committee that focuses on the issue addressed by the bill. In most legislatures, any school-related bill would be referred to the Education Committee.
- Before the full committee hears the bill, it might be considered by a subcommittee.
- The committee will make the decision about whether the bill will be approved for action by the full house, amended, defeated, tabled, or referred to a study committee.
- If the bill moves forward, it will be considered by the full chamber. It may be amended. It may be rereferred to another committee. (If the bill involves spending money, it may need to move through the appropriations, or budget, process.)
- Bills must be passed by both chambers, and if the language in the bills is not identical, a conference committee will have to work out any differences.
- Then the final bill goes to the governor, who can sign it, amend it and refer it back for further consideration, or veto it.

A bill can go off the rails at any one of these points. So getting legislation introduced on your behalf will need to be a priority for you and your family. Someone (OK, you) will have to spend time talking with legislators. Someone will need to be in the state capitol, probably several times.

Much of the advice on getting a district policy changed applies to getting a state law changed. But there are a few nuances.

Perhaps the best observation on the legislative process was offered by former president Lyndon Johnson: "The time to make friends is before you need them." Legislating depends on persuading people who probably don't know much about your issue to care about it. Relationships matter.

So get to know the individuals who represent you in your state legislature. Even if they are from a different party, you can often find common ground. Legislators like to take care of the requests of constituents.

And again, do not get angry. Your goal is to persuade the official to be on your side, so threats and bluster are just not very effective.

Once the bill is introduced, try to talk in person to the members of a subcommittee or committee that will consider your bill. That means you'll need to spend time in the state capitol building. Bring a one-page summary of your issue.

And watch the process. Bills get derailed in the dead of night. They get amended in ways that can essentially gut your efforts. You need to watch your bill at every step.

Even so, it's not likely to pass in its first year. State legislatures meet for a short period of time, and they consider lots of bills. Don't be discouraged if your effort doesn't bear fruit the first year.

One of the most successful long-term legislative strategies has been conducted by Mothers Against Drunk Driving. For more than a quarter century, MADD has worked with state legislators to raise the legal drinking age, lower the amount of alcohol drivers can have in their bloodstream, and prohibit young people from driving with any alcohol in their bloodstream. Over the years, MADD has helped change laws in dozens of states, resulting in a dramatic reduction in alcohol-related traffic deaths.

#81. SHOULD I SUE THE DISTRICT?

"If you never get sued, you probably aren't doing your job." That wise advice was given to me on my very first day as a school board member. (OK, it was given to me by a lawyer, but it was still wise advice.)

Look, we live in a litigious society. But if you're a parent trying to get the school board to change a decision you don't like, you should know how school boards view the threat of a lawsuit: mostly, they don't worry about it.

Still, parents persist in filing lawsuits to overturn school board decisions. There are times when parents are suing to protect their child's basic civil rights. Those lawsuits often need to be filed so that there is a legal basis for protecting the rights of a group that has been discriminated against.

It should be noted that courts generally are not interested in substituting their judgment for that of a duly elected (or appointed) body. As the Supreme Court noted in *Morse v. Frederick,* "School principals have a difficult job, and a vitally important one."[1] So, if the board has followed its policy and procedures in making a decision, and if those policies have been developed with a goal of maintaining students' constitutional rights (which is why school boards have good attorneys), a court is unlikely to overturn their decision.

Parents can, and often do, file lawsuits over things that courts are never going to decide. These include (and I am not making any of them up), lawsuits that asked courts to:

- overturn a coach's decision and place a student on the JV soccer team[2]
- overturn a suspension from school for a student who "mooned" a teacher[3]
- prohibit a calculus teacher from assigning work during the summer[4]

But although courts won't intervene in many school-based decisions, as the Supreme Court held in the case of *Tinker v. Des Moines Community School District,* "It can hardly be argued that either students or teachers shed their constitutional rights to freedom of speech or expression at the schoolhouse gate."[5] So parents who believe their child's constitutional rights have been violated will continue to file lawsuits to overturn school board decisions.

Although these cases can be very expensive, advocacy groups might be willing to represent your student at no charge to you. That's what happened when Gavin Grimm, a transgender student in Gloucester County, Virginia, sued his school board for the right to use the boys' bathroom.

The district had originally allowed Grimm to use that restroom. Like the school boards representing more than half of Virginia's public-school students, the Gloucester County board had no problems until news reports began to cover the story. At that point, complaints began, many made by people who did not live in the district.

So the school board created a new policy, promising to provide male and female restroom and locker room facilities in its schools. The policy spelled out that "the use of said facilities shall be limited to the corresponding biological genders." And while the board did not define "biological gender," it said it would rely on the sex marker on the student's birth certificate.[6]

Grimm then presented the board with an amended birth certificate from the Commonwealth of Virginia stating he was male. The board refused to accept it and instead, required him to use either the girl's restroom or an alternative restroom that was far from his classes. Using them caused him to be late to class. Grimm also felt that using these restrooms conveyed a stigma that was not applied to other students. So he sued.

The ACLU represented Grimm, and in 2020, a panel of judges on the U.S. Court of Appeals for the Fourth Circuit ruled in his favor. They said the board's policy violated the Equal Protection clause of the Fourteenth Amendment and Title IX of the Education Amendments of 1972.

In the decision, Judge Henry Floyd said that providing a segregated restroom for Grimm was not treating everyone equally. "[T]hat is like saying that racially segregated bathrooms treated everyone equally, because everyone was prohibited from using the bathroom of a different race. No one would suppose that also providing a "race neutral" bathroom option would have solved the deeply stigmatizing and discriminatory nature of racial segregation; so too here.[7]

Because the decision was made in a federal Court of Appeals, the Grimm family did not just change the policy for their son. They also changed it for transgender students in the entire Fourth Circuit: Virginia, Maryland, West Virginia, North Carolina, and South Carolina. (Just before this book was printed, the Gloucester County School Board announced they would appeal the Fourth Circuit decision to the Supreme Court.)

In other cases, parents have addressed problems affecting not only their own child, but many others as well. In one Tennessee case, parents learned that video equipment had been installed in the girls' and boys' locker rooms, and that school officials viewed and retained the recorded images. Charging that the policy violated the Fourth Amendment right to privacy, parents successfully sued in federal court to remove the equipment. The Sixth Circuit supported the parents.[8]

Similarly, an Arizona family sued their school district after learning that their middle school daughter had been subjected to a strip search at school after finding over-the-counter ibuprofen in another student's backpack. The other student implicated their daughter. searched. The Supreme Court ruled that the search was unconstitutional.[9]

So my advice is to think carefully before you file a lawsuit. It will take time, and many lawsuits are not resolved until after the student involved has graduated. It may come with a significant price tag unless an outside organization agrees to help. Still, if you are seeking relief for a violation of constitutional rights, a court case may well be your only alternative.

CONCLUSION

I was part of a group of parents who followed these steps more than 30 years ago, and it changed the trajectory of my life. Shortly after my daughter enrolled in elementary school, our school learned that every school in the district that had been built in 1952 would be renovated as a part of the 1988 school bond referendum. There was one exception—the school Sara attended.

Now, a renovation is not an insignificant thing for a school. It is a multimillion-dollar upgrade, providing the school with an inside-and-out refresh, new technology, and better use of space.

For a time, this school board decision was all that parents talked about at PTA meetings and on the sidelines of their kids' soccer games. It was during one of those conversations that I uttered the always fateful words: "Somebody ought to do something about it."

You can probably write the rest of the story. I got involved, along with many other parents. We started asking questions. Why had our school been left off the list? What would it take to get our school added? We lobbied and persuaded. Eventually, our school was added to the list of those that would be renovated with funds from the 1988 bond referendum.

Along the way, I decided that maybe what I really wanted was to be the person who would make decisions like that. That led to a seat on the school board. And that in turn led to a decade in the Virginia General Assembly.

So I give you fair warning that getting involved in an issue like this could change your life. Even if you don't end up on your local school board or running for the state legislature, you'll know a lot more about how your school and school district operate.

I never planned a career as a policymaker. I was a kindergarten volunteer and things got out of hand. But along the way, I asked a lot of questions. I learned a lot about how schools work. And now I hope you can take those lessons and use them to make things better not only for your child, but for all children.

NOTES

INTRODUCTION

1. Tennessee Department of Education. (2020, September 23). *Tennessee releases data showing significant learning loss among K–12 students.* Retrieved from https://www.tn.gov/governor/news/2020/9/23/tennessee-releases-data-showing-significant-learning-loss-among-k-12-students.html

2. Dreyer, B. (2019). *Dreyer's English: An utterly correct guide to clarity and style.* New York, NY: Random House, p. 93.

CHAPTER 1

1. Alexander, J. M., Johnson, K. E., Leibham, M. E., & Kelly, K. (2008). The development of conceptual interests in young children. *Cognitive Development, 23*(2),324-334.

2. Mageau, G. A., Vallerand, R. J., Charest, J., Salvy, S., Lacaille, N., Bouffard, T., & Koestner, R. (2009, June). On the development of harmonious and obsessive passion: The role of autonomy support, activity specialization, and identification with the activity. *Journal of Personality, 77*(3), 601–646.

3. Bloom, B. S. (1985). *Developing talent in young people.* New York, NY: Ballantine Books, p. 518.

4. Lythcott-Haims, J. (2015). *How to raise an adult: Break free of the overparenting trap and prepare your kid for success.* New York, NY: Henry Holt.

5. Michaeil Jordan's Basketball Hall of Fame Enshrinement Speech (2012, Feb. 21) https://www.youtube.com/watch?v=XLzBMGXfK4c

6. Gladwell, M. (2013, August 21). Complexity and the ten-thousand-hour rule. *The New Yorker.* Retrieved from https://www.newyorker.com/sports/sporting-scene/complexity-and-the-ten-thousand-hour-rule

7. Robinson, K. (2006, February). *How schools kill creativity* [Video file]. Retrieved from https://www.ted.com/talks/sir_ken_robinson_do_schools_kill_creativity

8. Anderson, M. W., & Johanson, T. D. (2013). *GIST: The essence of raising life-ready kids*. Eden Prairie, MN: GISTWorks.

9. Levine, M. (2020). *Ready or not: Preparing our kids to thrive in an uncertain and rapidly changing world*. New York, NY: HarperCollins.

10. Levine, M. (2012). *Teach your children well: Why values and coping skills matter more than grades, trophies, or "fat envelopes."* New York, NY: HarperCollins.

11. Iowa State University. (2017). *Futurity: Putting a TV in your kid's bedroom carries risks*. Retrieved from https://www.futurity.org/television-childrens-bedrooms-1555172-2/

12. American Academy of Pediatrics. (2016). *Media and young minds*. Retrieved from www.aap.org

13. Winther, D. K. (2020). *Rethinking screen time in the time of COVID-19*. UNICEF Office of Global Insight and Policy. Retrieved from https://www.unicef.org/globalinsight/stories/rethinking-screen-time-time-covid-19

14. Gentile, D. A., Berch, O. N., Choo, H., Khoo, A., & Walsh, D. A. (2017). Bedroom media: One risk factor for development. *Developmental Psychology, 53*(12), 2340–2355. Retrieved from https://doi.org/10.1037/dev0000399

15. Jiang, J. (2018). *How teens and parents navigate screen time and device distractions*. Pew Research Center. Retrieved from https://www.pewresearch.org/internet/2018/08/22/how-teens-and-parents-navigate-screen-time-and-device-distractions/

16. Henderson, A. T., & Berla, N. (1994). *A new generation of evidence: The family is critical to student achievement*. Washington, DC: National Committee for Citizens in Education.

17. Marcon, R. A. (1999). Positive relationships between parent school involvement and public school inner-city preschoolers' development and academic performance. *School Psychology Review, 28*(3), 395–412.

18. Sheff, D. (1988, January 19). Opinion: "Izzy, did you ask a good question today?" *The New York Times*.

19. American Experience, PBS. (n.d.). *Mary Pinkney Hardy MacArthur*. Retrieved from https://www.pbs.org/wgbh/americanexperience/features/macarthur-mary-pinkney-hardy-macarthur/

20. Indiana University. (2007). *"Helicopter parents" stir up anxiety, depression*. Retrieved from http://newsinfo.iu.edu/web/page/normal/6073.html

21. Lythcott-Haims, *How to raise an adult*, p. 59.

22. Mathews, J. (2007, October 16). Ten stupid ways to ruin your college application. *The Washington Post*. Retrieved from http://www.washingtonpost.com/wp-dyn/content/article/2007/10/16/AR2007101600543.html?hpid=news-col-blog

23. Morin, A. (2017, August 20). Parents, please don't attend your adult child's job interview. *Forbes*. Retrieved from https://www.forbes.com/sites/

amymorin/2017/08/29/parents-please-dont-attend-your-adult-childs-job-interview/#579bb

24. Chang, H. N., & Romero, M. (2008). *Present, engaged, and accounted for: The critical importance of addressing chronic absence in the early grades.* Washington, DC: National Center for Children in Poverty. Retrieved from http://www.nccp.org/publications/pdf/text_837.pdf

25. Baltimore Education Research Consortium. (2011). *Destination graduation: Sixth grade early warning indicators for Baltimore City Schools.* Retrieved from http://www.baltimore-berc.org/pdfs/SixthGradeEWIFullReport.pdf

26. Office of Juvenile Justice and Delinquency Prevention, Model Programs Guide. (n.d.). *Truancy prevention.* Retrieved from http://www.ojjdp.gov/mpg/Topic/Details/122

CHAPTER 2

1. Lake, R. (2020, April 30). *Flattening the learning loss curve when school reopens will take federal leadership, state and local buy-in and these 4 steps.* Retrieved from https://www.the74million.org/article/robin-lake-flattening-the-learning-loss-curve-when-school-reopens-will-take-federal-leadership-state-and-local-buy-in-and-these-4-steps/

2. Miles, K. H. (2020, July 30). *Remote school is back: Here's how leaders can organize resources to make remote teaching and learning work.* Retrieved from https://www.erstrategies.org/news/remote_school_is_back

3. Fickman, L. (2020, March 31). *Remote learning requires new lessons for parents and teachers.* Retrieved from https://uh.edu/news-events/stories/2020/march-2020/03312020-remote-learning-new-lessons-parents-teachers.php

4. Wright, W. (2020, August 8). No pajama pants allowed while learning from home, Illinois district says. *The New York Times.* Retrieved from https://www.nytimes.com/2020/08/08/us/pajamas-school-springfield-dress-code.html

5. Hainey, M. (2016, April 26). Lin-Manuel Miranda thinks the key to parenting is a little less parenting. *GQ Magazine.* Retrieved from https://www.gq.com/story/unexpected-lin-manuel-miranda

6. Paul, P. (2019, February 2). Let children get bored again. *The New York Times.* Retrieved from https://www.nytimes.com/2019/02/02/opinion/sunday/children-bored.html

7. Alliance for Excellent Education. (2020). *Students of color caught in the homework gap.* Retrieved from https://futureready.org/homework-gap/

8. Chandra, S., Chang, A., Day, L., Fazlullah, A., Liu, J., McBride, L., Mudalige, T., & Weiss, D. (2020). *Closing the K–12 digital divide in the age of distance learning.* San Francisco, CA: Common Sense Media. Boston, MA: Boston Consulting Group. Retrieved from https://www.commonsensemedia.org/sites/default/files/uploads/pdfs/common_sense_media_report_final_7_1_3pm_web.pdf

9. Ander, R., Guryan, J., & Ludwig, J. (2020, 16 March). *Improving academic outcomes for disadvantaged students: Scaling up individual tutorials.* The Hamilton Project. Retrieved from https://www.hamiltonproject.org/assets/files/improving_academic_outcomes_for_disadvantaged_students_pp.pdf

10. Harden, N. (2020, May 29). *COVID-19's surprise effect: More parents are interested in home schooling.* RealClear Education. Retrieved from https://www.realcleareducation.com/articles/2020/05/29/covid-19s_surprise_effect_more_parents_are_interested_in_home_schooling_110425.html

11. National Public Radio. (2014, January 14). *As a Latina, Sonia Sotomayor says, "You have to work harder."* Fresh air with Terry Gross [Radio broadcast]. Retrieved from https://www.wkms.org/post/latina-sonia-sotomayor-says-you-have-work-harder#stream/0

12. Strauss, V. (2012, December 5). List: What Common Core authors suggest high schoolers should read. The Answer Sheet. *The Washington Post.* Retrieved from https://www.washingtonpost.com/news/answer-sheet/wp/2012/12/05/list-what-common-core-authors-suggest-high-schoolers-should-read/

13. Aspen Institute. (2020). *#Disconnected: Covid-19 and the digital divide.* Retrieved from https://assets.aspeninstitute.org/content/uploads/2020/04/Aspen-DigitalDivide-Slides_Larry-Irving.pdf

14. Anderson, M., & Kumar, M. (2019). *Digital divide persists even as lower-income Americans make gains in tech adoption.* Pew Research Center. Retrieved from https://www.pewresearch.org/fact-tank/2019/05/07/digital-divide-persists-even-as-lower-income-americans-make-gains-in-tech-adoption/

CHAPTER 3

1. Educationdata.org. (2019). *K-12 school enrollment and student population statistics.* Retrieved from https://educationdata.org/k12-enrollment-statistics/

2. Hutton, L. (2012). *I did it all by myself: An age-by-age guide to teaching your child life skills.* Family Education Network. Retrieved from https://www.familyeducation.com/life/individuality/guide-to-teach-your-child-life-skills-by-age

3. National Center for Education Statistics. (2013). *Kindergarten entry status: On-time, delayed-entry, and repeating kindergarteners.* Retrieved from https://nces.ed.gov/programs/coe/indicator_tea.asp

4. Schanzenbach, D. W., & Larson, S. L. (2017, April). Is your child ready for kindergarten? *Education Next, 17*(3). Retrieved from https://www.educationnext.org/is-your-child-ready-kindergarten-redshirting-may-do-more-harm-than-good/

5. Elder, T. E., & Lubotsky, D. H. (2009, Summer). Kindergarten entrance age and children's achievement: Impacts of state policies, family background, and peers. *Journal of Human Resources, 44*(3), 641–683.

6. Dennis, J. (2008, August 18). *Study: Starting kindergarten later gives students only a fleeting edge.* Illinois News Bureau, University of Illinois at Urbana-Champaign. Retrieved from https://news.illinois.edu/view/6367/206218

7. Byrd, R. S., Weitzman, M., & Auinger, P. (1997). Increased behavior problems associated with delayed school entry and delayed school progress. *Pediatrics, 100*(4), 654–661.

8. Graue, M. E., & DiPerna, J. (2000). Redshirting and early retention: Who gets the "gift of time" and what are its outcomes? *American Educational Research Journal, 37*(2), 509–534.

9. Nord, C. W., Lennon, J., Liu, B., & Chandler, K. (1999). *Home literacy activities and signs of children's emerging literacy, 1993 and 1999.* Washington, DC: U.S. Department of Education, National Center for Education Statistics.

10. Munzer, T. G., Miller, A. L., Weeks, H. M., Kaciroti, N., & Radesky, J. (2019, April). Differences in parent-toddler interactions with electronic versus print books. *Pediatrics, 143*(4). Retrieved from https://pediatrics.aappublications.org/content/143/4/e20182012

11. *ScienceDaily.* (2018, December 3). University of British Columbia. Science News. Importance of good sleep routines for children. Retrieved from https://www.sciencedaily.com/releases/2018/12/181203080327.htm

CHAPTER 4

1. Levine, M. (2012). *Teach your children well: Why values and coping skills matter more than grades, trophies, or "fat envelopes."* New York, NY: HarperCollins.

2. Dufur, M. J., Parcel, T. L., & Troutman, K. P. (2013). Does capital at home matter more than capital at school? Social capital effects on academic achievement. *Research in Social Stratification and Mobility, 31*, 1–21.

3. Hernandez, D. J. (2012). *Double jeopardy: How third-grade reading skills and poverty influence high school graduation.* Baltimore, MD: Annie E. Casey Foundation. Retrieved from https://www.aecf.org/resources/double-jeopardy/

4. Finkel, D. (2015, November). *5 ways to share math with kids* [Video file]. TedXRanier. Retrieved from https://www.ted.com/talks/dan_finkel_5_ways_to_share_math_with_kids/transcript?language=en

5. Heath, C., & Heath, D. (2010). *Switch: How to change things when change is hard.* New York, NY: Broadway Books.

6. Lythcott-Haims, J. (2015). *How to raise an adult: Break free of the overparenting trap and prepare your kid for success.* New York, NY: Henry Holt.

CHAPTER 5

1. Lythcott-Haims, J. (2015). *How to raise an adult: Break free of the overparenting trap and prepare your kid for success.* New York, NY: Henry Holt.

2. Rosenbaum, J. E. (2004). What you need to do in high school if you want to graduate from college. *American Educator, 28*(1), 8–10.

3. Achieve. (2008). *Building blocks of success: Higher level math for all students.* Retrieved from https://www.achieve.org/publications/building-blocks-success-higher-level-math-all-students

4. Rosenbaum, What you need to do, pp. 8–10.

5. Roth, J., Crans, G. G., Carter, R. L., Ariet, M., & Resnick, M. B. (2000). Effect of high school course-taking and grades on passing a college placement test. *High School Journal, 84*(2), 72.

6. U.S. Department of Education, Office of Civil Rights. (2018). *2015–16 Civil rights data collection: STEM course taking.* Retrieved from https://www2.ed.gov/about/offices/list/ocr/docs/stem-course-taking.pdf

7. National Council of Teachers of English. (2018). *A call to action: What we know about adolescent literacy instruction.* Retrieved from https://ncte.org/statement/adolescentliteracy/

8. Linville, D., Stice, E., Gau, J., & O'Neil, M. (2011). Predictive effects of mother and peer influences on increases in adolescent eating disorder risk factors and symptoms: A 3-year longitudinal study. *International Journal of Eating Disorders, 44*(8), 745–751. Retrieved from https://onlinelibrary.wiley.com/doi/epdf/10.1002/eat.20907

9. Steinberg, L. (2011). *Adolescence.* New York, NY: McGraw-Hill, p. 291.

10. Fisman, R. (2010, May 12). The right kind of peer pressure. *Slate.* Retrieved from https://slate.com/business/2010/05/want-girls-to-do-better-in-school-surround-them-with-smart-classmates.html

11. Robb, M. (2019). *Tweens, teens, and phones: What our 2019 research reveals.* Common Sense Media. Retrieved from https://www.commonsensemedia.org/blog/tweens-teens-and-phones-what-our-2019-research-reveals

12. Somers, P., & Settle, J. (2010). The helicopter parent (part 2): International arrivals and departures. *College and University, 86*(2). Retrieved from https://www.aacrao.org/docs/default-source/c-u-.pdfs/cuj8602_web.pdf?sfvrsn=81f5e85a_0

13. Anderson, M. (2016, January 7). *6 takeaways about how parents monitor their teen's digital activities.* Pew Research Center. Retrieved from https://www.pewresearch.org/fact-tank/2016/01/07/parents-teens-digital-monitoring/

14. Anderson, M. (2018). *A majority of teens have experienced some form of cyberbullying. Pew Research Center.* Retrieved from https://www.pewresearch.org/internet/2018/09/27/a-majority-of-teens-have-experienced-some-form-of-cyberbullying/

15. Levine, M. (2012). *Teach your children well: Why values and coping skills mattter more than grades, trophies, or "fat envelopes."* New York, NY: HarperCollins, p. 134.

16. John, A., Glendenning, A. C., Marchant, A., Montgomery, P., Stewart, A., Wood, S., Lloyd, K., & Hawton, K. (2018). Self-harm, suicidal behaviours, and cyberbullying in children and young people: Systematic review. *Journal of Medical Internet Research, 20*(4), e129.

17. Anderson, *A majority of teens.*

18. John et al., Self-harm, suicidal behaviours.

CHAPTER 6

1. American Academy of Child and Adolescent Psychiatry. (2016). *Teen brain: Behavior, problem solving and decision making.* Retrieved from https://www.aacap. org/AACAP/Families_and_Youth/Facts_for_Families/FFF-Guide/The-Teen-Brain-Behavior-Problem-Solving-and-Decision-Making-095.aspx

2. Guhn, M., Emerson, S. D., & Gouzouasis, P. (2020). A population-level analysis of associations between school music participation and academic achievement. *Journal of Educational Psychology, 112*(2), 308–328. Retrieved from https://doi.org/10.1037/edu0000376

3. Chute, E. (1999, August 28). Back to school: Scheduling can be a monumental task. *Pittsburgh Post-Gazette.* Retrieved from https://old.post-gazette.com/regionstate/19990828schedule2.asp

4. Youth Truth. (2016). *Learning from student voice: College and career readiness.* Retrieved from https://youthtruthsurvey.org/college-and-career-readiness/

5. Hart Research Associates. (2011, August 18). *One year out: Findings from a national survey among members of the high graduating class of 2010.* Retrieved from https://secure-media.collegeboard.org/homeOrg/content/pdf/One_Year_Out_key_findings%20report_final.pdf

6. New Trier High School. (2020). *4 steps to the future: Post high school planning guide.* Retrieved from https://newtrier.k12.il.us/phsc/

7. Patrick, K., Socol, A. R., & Morgan, I. (2020, January 9). *Inequities in advanced coursework.* The Education Trust. Retrieved from https://edtrust.org/resource/inequities-in-advanced-coursework/

8. College Board. (2020). *AP program results: Class of 2019.* Retrieved from https://reports.collegeboard.org/ap-program-results

9. Theokas, C. (2013). *Finding America's missing AP and IB students.* The Education Trust. Retrieved from https://edtrust.org/resource/finding-americas-missing-ap-and-ib-students/

10. Patrick, Socol, & Morgan, *Inequities in advanced coursework.*

11. Fink, J., Jenkins, D., & Yanagiura, T. (2017). *What happens to students who take community college "dual enrollment" classes in high school?* Teachers College, Columbia University, Community College Research Center. Retrieved from https://ccrc.tc.columbia.edu/media/k2/attachments/what-happens-community-college-dual-enrollment-students.pdf

12. U.S. Department of Education. (2017). *Issue brief: Academic tutoring in high schools.* Retrieved from https://www2.ed.gov/rschstat/eval/high-school/academic-tutoring.pdf

13. National Collegiate Athletic Association. (2020). *Estimated probability of competing in college athletics*. Retrieved from http://www.ncaa.org/about/resources/research/estimated-probability-competing-college-athletics

14. Fulks, B. (2017). *X-plan: Giving your kids a way out (#xplan)*. Retrieved from https://bertfulks.com/2017/02/23/x-plan-giving-your-kids-a-way-out-xplan/

15. National Center for Missing and Exploited Children. (2009). *Policy statement on sexting*. Retrieved from www.missingkids.com/home

16. Anderson, M. (2018). *A majority of teens have experienced some form of cyberbullying*. Pew Research Center. Retrieved from https://www.pewresearch.org/internet/2018/09/27/a-majority-of-teens-have-experienced-some-form-of-cyberbullying/

17. Anderson, *A majority of teens*.

18. Geiger, A. W. (2018). *Q&A: How and why we studied teens and cyberbullying*. Pew Research Center. Retrieved from https://www.pewresearch.org/fact-tank/2018/09/27/qa-how-and-why-we-studied-teens-and-cyberbullying/

19. Strasburger, V. C., Zimmerman, H., Temple, J. R., & Madigan, S. (2019, May). Teenagers, sexting and the law. *Pediatrics, 143*(5), e20183183.

20. Madigan, S., Van Ouytsel, J., & Temple, J. R. (2018). Nonconsensual sexting and the role of sex differences—reply. *JAMA Pediatrics, 172*(9), 890–891.

21. Teresa L. Morisi, "Teen labor force participation before and after the Great Recession and beyond," *Monthly Labor Review*, U.S. Bureau of Labor Statistics, February 2017. Retrieved from https://doi.org/10.21916/mlr.2017.5.

22. Kelly, K. (1998, July/August). Working teenagers: Do after-school jobs hurt? *Harvard Education Letter, 14*(4). Retrieved from https://www.hepg.org/hel-home/issues/14_4/helarticle/working-teenagers_343

23. The Institute for College Access and Success. (2020, July). *What college can cost for low-income Californians, 2020*. Retrieved from https://ticas.org/wp-content/uploads/2020/08/what-college-costs-for-low-income-californians-2020.pdf

CHAPTER 7

1. Carnevale, A. P., Strohl, J., Ridley, R., & Gulish, A. *Three educational pathways to good jobs: High school, middle skills, and bachelor's degree*. Washington, DC: Georgetown University Center on Education and the Workforce, 2018.

2. Politico, Morning Education. (2018). *SAT scores rise, as do the numbers of test-takers*. Retrieved from https://www.politico.com/newsletters/morning-education/2018/10/25/sat-scores-rise-as-do-the-numbers-of-test-takers-388387

3. University of Chicago. (2020). *Applications: Frequently asked questions*. Retrieved from https://collegeadmissions.uchicago.edu/contact/frequently-asked-questions

4. Keilman, J. (2020, August 10). COVID-19 shutdowns create mad dash for ACT, SAT spots as college application season looms. *Chicago Tribune*. Retrieved

from https://www.chicagotribune.com/coronavirus/ct-act-sat-coronavirus-covid-college-application-20200810-4orfahifyzh4ff34tsteh2h7o4-story.html

5. George Mason University. (2020). *How to apply.* Retrieved from https://www2.gmu.edu/admissions-aid/how-apply/freshman

6. Narayanan, S. L., & Srivastava, D. B. (2020). The class of 2023, academics and extracurriculars. *The Harvard Crimson.* Retrieved from https://features.thecrimson.com/2019/freshman-survey/academics-narrative/

7. Lewin, T. (2006, August 31). Students' paths to small colleges can bypass SAT. *The New York Times.* https://www.nytimes.com/2006/08/31/education/31sat.html

8. Belkin, D. (2015, January 9). Colleges turn to personality assessments to find successful students. *Wall Street Journal.* https://www.wsj.com/articles/colleges-turn-to-personality-assessments-to-find-successful-students-1420762583

9. Blake, A. (2015, January 30). Where the Senate went to college—in one map. *The Washington Post.* https://www.washingtonpost.com/news/the-fix/wp/2015/01/30/where-the-senate-went-to-college-in-one-map/

10. Moody, J. (2020, June 10). Where the top Fortune 500 CEOs attended college. *U.S. News & World Report.* https://www.usnews.com/education/best-colleges/articles/where-the-top-fortune-500-ceos-attended-college

11. Bruni, F. (2015). *Where you go is not who you'll be: An antidote to the college admissions mania.* New York, NY: Grand Central, 66.

12. Boughton, C. (2008, August 31). Personal interview.

CHAPTER 8

1. Cooper, H., Robinson, J. C., & Patall, E. A. (2006). Does homework improve academic achievement? A synthesis of research, 1987–2003. *Review of Educational Research, 76*(1), 1–62.

2. Rosenbaum, J. E. (2004). It's time to tell the kids: If you don't do well in high school, you won't do well in college (or on the job). *American Educator, 28*(1), 8–10.

3. Bennett, S., & Kalish, N. (2006). *The case against homework: How homework is hurting our children and what we can do about it.* New York, NY: Crown.

4. Kralovic, E., & Buell, J. (2001, April). End homework now. *Educational Leadership, 58*(7). Retrieved from http://www.ascd.org/publications/educational-leadership/apr01/vol58/num07/End-Homework-Now.aspx

5. Rideout, V., & Robb, M. B. (2019). *The Common Sense census: Media use by tweens and teens, 2019.* San Francisco, CA: Common Sense Media.

6. Zernicke, K. (2000, October 10). As homework load grows, one district says enough. *The New York Times.* Retrieved from https://www.nytimes.com/2000/10/10/nyregion/as-homework-load-grows-one-district-says-enough.html

7. Piscataway, New Jersey, Schools. (2019). *No homework night flyer.* Retrieved from https://piscatawayschools.org/district_/news/what_s_new/no_homework_night

8. Education Endowment Foundation. (2020). *Evidence summaries: Teaching and learning toolkit, primary homework.* Retrieved from https://educationendowment-foundation.org.uk/evidence-summaries/teaching-learning-toolkit/homework-primary/

9. Education Endowment Foundation. (2020). *Evidence summaries: Teaching and learning toolkit, secondary homework.* Retrieved from https://education endowmentfoundation.org.uk/evidence-summaries/teaching-learning-toolkit/homework-secondary/

10. May, C. (2018, May 29). The problem with "learning styles." *Scientific American,* Behavior and Society. Retrieved from https://www.scientificamerican.com/article/the-problem-with-learning-styles/

11. Lamott, A. (1994). *Bird by bird: Some instructions on writing and life.* New York, NY: Random House, pp. 18–19.

12. National Center for Education Statistics. (2017). *Percentage of elementary and secondary school students who do homework, average time spent doing homework, percentage whose parents check that homework is done, and percentage whose parents help with homework, by frequency and selected characteristics: 2007, 2012, and 2016.* Retrieved from https://nces.ed.gov/programs/digest/d17/tables/dt17_227.40.asp

13. Rideout, V. J., Foehr, U. G., & Roberts, D. F. (2010). *Generation M2: Media in the lives of 8- to 18-year-olds.* Menlo Park, CA: Kaiser Family Foundation.

14. Stavrinos, D., McManus, B., Underhill, A. T., & Lechtreck, M. T. (2019, April). Impact of adolescent media multitasking on cognition and driving safety. *Human Behavior and Emerging Technologies, 1*(2), 161–168.

15. American Psychological Association. (2006). *Multitasking: Switching costs.* Retrieved from https://www.apa.org/research/action/multitask

16. Reid, K. S. (2013, September 18). Survey finds half of parents struggle with their children's homework. *Education Week,* Families and the Community. Retrieved from https://blogs.edweek.org/edweek/parentsandthepublic/2013/09/half_of_parents_struggle_to_help_their_kids_with_homework_survey_finds.html

17. Pashler, H., McDaniel, M., Rohrer, D., & Bjork, R. A. (2008). Learning styles: Concepts and evidence. *Psychological Science in the Public Interest, 9*(3), 105–119.

18. Willingham, D. (2018, October 4). Are you a visual or an auditory learner? It doesn't matter. *The New York Times.*

19. Willingham, Are you a visual or an auditory learner?

20. Dweck, C. S. (2015, September 22). Carol Dweck revisits the "growth mindset." *Education Week,* Student Well Being—Commentary. Retrieved from https://www.edweek.org/leadership/opinion-carol-dweck-revisits-the-growth-mindset/2015/09

21. Ericsson, K. A., Charness, N., Feltovich, P. J., & Hoffman, R. R. (Eds.). (2006). *The Cambridge Handbook of Expertise and Expert Performance*. New York, NY: Cambridge University Press.

22. Whitman, G., & Kelleher, I. (2016). *Neuro teach: Brain science and the future of education*. Lanham, MD: Rowman & Littlefield.

23. Whitman & Kelleher, *Neuro teach*, p. 49.

24. Kang, S. H. K. (2016). Spaced repetition promotes efficient and effective learning: Policy implications for instruction. *Policy Insights from the Behavioral and Brain Sciences, 3*(1), 12–19. Retrieved from https://www.dartmouth.edu/~cogedlab/pubs/Kang(2016,PIBBS).pdf

25. Hartwig, M. K., & Dunlosky, J. (2012). Study strategies of college students: Are self-testing and scheduling related to achievement? *Psychonomic Bulletin & Review, 19*(1), 126–134. Retrieved from https://doi.org/10.3758/s13423-011-0181-y

26. Hartwig & Dunlosky, Study strategies.

CHAPTER 9

1. *Morse v. Frederick,* 551 U.S. 393 (2007).

2. Kim Bell and Robert Patrick, (2018, October 2). "Parents sue school district after son doesn't make soccer team; suit blames age discrimination," *St. Louis Post-Dispatch.*

3. Thomas C. Tobin, (2007, April 13). "Parents sue to get student reinstated," *Tampa Bay Times.*

4. *Larson v. Burmaster,* 720 N.W.2d 134 (2006).

5. *Tinker v. Des Moines Community School District*, 393 U.S. 503 (1969).

6. *Grimm v. Gloucester County School Board*, 972 F.3d 586, 608 (4th Cir. 2020) (No. 19-1952).

7. Id at 609.

8. Brannum v. Overton County School Board, 516 F.3d 489 (6th Cir. 2008) (No. 06-5931).

9. Redding v. Safford Unified Sch. Dist. #1, 557 U.S. 364 (2009).

ABOUT THE AUTHOR

Kristen J. Amundson has more than three decades of leadership in K–12 education at the local, state, and national levels. She served as the president and CEO of the National Association of State Boards of Education from 2013 to 2019.

Amundson represented the 44th District in the Virginia General Assembly from 1999 to 2009. She was vice chair of the House Democratic Caucus and served as its political director. During that time, she was a member of Virginia's P–16 Council and the Southern Regional Education Board (SREB).

Before her election to the General Assembly, Amundson—a former teacher—served for nearly a decade on the Fairfax County, Virginia, school board, including two years as its chairwoman. She was the senior vice president for external affairs at Education Sector, an independent think tank.

She has written extensively about parenting. Her publications include *Kids Don't Come With Instruction Manuals* and *Getting Your Child Ready for Kindergarten*. She is a frequent author of opinion pieces on education and has been published in the *Richmond Times-Dispatch* and *The Washington Post*, among others.

Fifteen years ago, with two friends, she cofounded La BECA Women's Scholarship Foundation. Since then, La BECA has provided support to more than 100 girls and women in Central and South America to pursue their educational dreams. In 2020, in the midst of the COVID-19 crisis that shut schools across Virginia, she cofounded EduTutorVA, a nonprofit organization to link trained tutors with Virginia's lowest-achieving students to help them close learning gaps. In 2021, she received the Distinguished Citizen Award from Macalester College, her alma mater.